Blind Perceptions

Blind Perceptions

Sociopolitical Psychology
and its
Impact on Civilization

Dean Kalahar

iUniverse, Inc.
New York Lincoln Shanghai

Blind Perceptions
Sociopolitical Psychology and its Impact on Civilization

iUniverse books may be ordered through booksellers or by contacting:

iUniverse
2021 Pine Lake Road, Suite 100
Lincoln, NE 68512
www.iuniverse.com
1-800-Authors (1-800-288-4677)

ISBN-13: 978-0-595-35992-9 (pbk)
ISBN-13: 978-0-595-80443-6 (ebk)
ISBN-10: 0-595-35992-2 (pbk)
ISBN-10: 0-595-80443-8 (ebk)

Printed in the United States of America

For Courtney

Contents

PREFACE ix

Part I   *OVERVIEW AND ANALYSIS OF CONFLICT*

CHAPTER 1   FOUNDATIONS 5

CHAPTER 2   WORLDVIEWS AND THE DECLINE OF
             MODERN CIVILIZATION 16

Part II   *WORLDVIEW DEVELOPMENT*

CHAPTER 3   MORALITY. 25

CHAPTER 4   NEEDS. 37

CHAPTER 5   LEARNING. 45

CHAPTER 6   POWER 56

CHAPTER 7   LEADERSHIP 63

CHAPTER 8   THEOLOGY. 68

CHAPTER 9   HUMAN NATURE 76

CHAPTER 10   NATURE 84

Part III   *APPLICATION*

CHAPTER 11   INSTITUTIONS AND CIVILIZATION 95

CHAPTER 12   GOVERNMENT 104

CHAPTER 13   ECONOMY 112

CHAPTER 14   EDUCATION 122

CHAPTER 15   FAMILY 129

CHAPTER 16   RELIGION. 135

Part IV   *DECISIONS*

CHAPTER 17   SUMMARY AND CONCLUSIONS. 145

PREFACE

This text focuses on how worldviews are developed and applied to the social institutions of civilized society. The purpose is to answer four questions. 1. Why do some people see the world in one way while others see it from a totally opposite perspective? 2. Why do worldviews change within individuals as they move through the developmental process? 3.What impact does one's world perspective have on their interpretation of social institutions? 4. What result will the application of binary world visions have on civilization?

The reason for undertaking such a journey stems from the fact that after twenty years of teaching it has become abundantly clear that citizens are confused and hopelessly misinformed as to the fundamental basis for their thoughts and actions. This in turn has created behaviors and institutional policy that is counterproductive to the advancement of civilization. In other words, the blind perceptions that dominate our culture inhibit the maintenance of civilization.

Everyone has a general feeling or understanding as to why they think as they do; but more often than not, the application of an individual's worldview is a hit and miss proposition. Because of this, our daily relationship with the society to which we belong is being guided not by clear thinking and intellectual consistency but by an emotionally charged mentality. Self interest and mixed messages that are intertwined into our thought processes from political demagogues and the media keep most of us from formulating a definitive understanding of self and our role in the world. This in turn create decision making processes that are not in the best interest of maintaining the health and vigor that our social institutions need to advance in a positive direction.

The theories discussed in this text have been around for as long as man has been pondering his existence. My attempt is to package them in a way that the average citizen can increase their understanding of the dynamic nature of worldviews and their application on the vital social institutions that hold civilization together. What is new is the analysis of how world visions are developed and transformed. Through a step by step look into some vital components of human cognitive growth, understanding and perception, a clear picture will emerge regarding worldview development. Hopefully, the end result will allow one to determine what processes have guided them into one of the binary worldviews.

Why does the general public often ignore this topic? The reason is because those who do discuss sociopolitical psychology often speak a language beyond the normal vernacular. This text however, is not a deep philosophical treatise on an intellectual plane far above the average person. In fact, it is designed to be user friendly for anyone who wants to better understand what they believe and why they believe it. With that said, any cognitive adventure worth pursuing will, as a necessity, have a base of critical of thought and analysis; but the purpose of the text is to actually have the reader grow intellectually. The intent is not to bore and talk over one's head, the goal is to guide you in a fashion that is understandable, enlightening and hopefully entertaining.

It is paramount to remember that others have said these things before and warned us of the dangers that intellectual confusion applied to the maintenance of our civilization can create. Therefore, the many quotes used to eloquently describe theories or points of view will hopefully give weight to the arguments that follow. The methodology is to give credit to the individual scholar at each and every point in the text where their thoughts and theories have been cited.

One will quickly identify with one of the two worldviews presented. Caution should be taken so that you do not close your mind because you decide to take a point being made personally. Personal growth is sometimes a difficult undertaking and it is important to keep an open mind and read with reason.

Many of you will experience cognitive dissonance as you read which may have you react in a way that all but ends the discussion. The specifics of cognitive dissonance theory will be discussed later in the text. It is hoped that readers will push forward and test their assumptions as well as their worldview.

It must also be mentioned that Thomas Sowell has discussed at length the application of world visions and it is not my intention to restate his thoughts. If you are interested in a more detailed examination of his intricate philosophy I would recommend you read: A Conflict of Visions and The Vision of the Anointed. These books will describe and apply binary visions to a myriad of topics.

With all of that said, let's begin our look into how the cognitive developmental process creates a perceptual model that defines how individuals view the world.

Dean Kalahar

This book would not have been possible without help from a number of extraordinary people who gave their time, energy, support and considerable skills. Thank you and sincere gratitude to: Mark Georgiades, Bob and Carol Scherer, Geri Carter and to every student and academic who challenged me to grow intellectually and as a person. Most importantly, much love to my wife for putting up with me and this project.

I

OVERVIEW AND ANALYSIS OF CONFLICT

All of us have sat across the dinner table and had a discussion with loved ones that turned emotional because one opinion came to odds with another. In fact, we can look at almost any aspect of everyday life and see examples of people debating the merits or demerits of every conceivable topic. In social, economic, parental, religious, educational and political avenues it seems that everyone has an opinion. More often than not those opinions fall into two diametrically opposite camps with each side unable to comprehend how and why the other perceives the topic from a different point of view. The end result is usually frustration, argument, emotion and eventually anger towards our fellow man.

Why is there a tendency for man to develop into one of two distinct types of perceptual models each with a polar opposite perspective on how they view the world? Where does man's peculiar inclination of finding two sides to every issue originate? Why can one's worldview transform from one set of assumptions and perceptions to the opposite set over time?

These questions on their own would be an interesting venue to explore if our only differences of opinion were with such banal questions as "who is the best rock band of all time?" Unfortunately, our deeply seated differences intersect and come into play regarding a myriad of highly important issues that impact everyone. Binary worldviews are applied by all of us to aspects of our civilization that are vital to our survival. Because of this interplay, decisions and assumptions are applied that have long lasting and significant ramifications. History is full of examples of great civilizations that have come and gone because the humans that enjoyed their fruits and were entrusted to their survival were unaware of their fragility. One of the primary reasons for the collapse of great societies has been the influence of blind perceptions that were applied to the maintenance of civilization.

Clearly we need a greater understanding of what our worldviews signify and from where our visions originate. Any meaningful journey would not be complete however, unless we sought to understand how we apply our worldviews to the institutions of our civilization and the vital questions of our time. Debate and discussion is wonderful, but blindly following one's worldview without a clue as to where it originates is dangerous, not only to ourselves but to the generations that hopefully will follow. If we better understand what we think, we will be able to work towards advancement of the civilization in lieu of working ignorantly towards its demise.

Why should we strive to understand our worldview? Erich Fromm touched on the blind perceptions of accepting limited ideologies instead of evaluating diverse visions in the quest for cognitive development: "Once a doctrine, however irrational, has gained power in a society, millions of people will believe in it rather than feel ostracized and isolated." The reason why people fail to grow beyond the role of follower is because to do so takes time and effort. This lack of effort causes intellectual apathy and is a primary cause of social confusion. John Adams also offered thoughts on perceptual blindness:

> Facts are stubborn things; and whatever may be our wishes, our inclinations, or the dictates of our passions, they cannot alter the state of facts and evidence. Men find ways to persuade themselves to believe any absurdity, to submit to any prostitution, rather than to forgo their wishes and desires. Their reason becomes at last an eloquent advocate on the side of their passions and (they) bring themselves to believe that black is white, that vice is virtue, that folly is wisdom, and eternity a moment.

John Locke, the enlightened father of our forefathers, expressed two fundamental reasons why man needs to further his understanding of the world and clarify the worldviews that guide behavior. "The improvement of understanding is for two ends: first, our own increase of knowledge; second, to enable us to deliver that knowledge to others." Locke also stated that: "A man may live long, and die at last in ignorance of many truths, which his mind was capable of knowing and that with certainty."

Hopefully this text can act as a tour guide to self discovery and intellectual leadership that will give rise to some personal reflection and possibly a reordering of perceptions of how you view the world. The realization of your worldview should offer a higher level of cognitive understanding and provide for more productive, empathetic and intuitive social discourse. The mental journey outlined can only be beneficial, however, if one takes the path of open mindedness. Arnold J. Toynbee outlined the personal growth process that we all must go through if we are to fully understand our worldviews:

> Introspection has two possible alternative objections. It may be a retreat into one's self from contact with other people and with the universe, or it may be a search, in the subconscious depths of the psyche, for contact with the ultimate spiritual reality. Introspection with the first of these objectives is isolationist; introspection with the second objective is unitive. The first is negative, the second is positive.

Lastly, Carl Jung stated: "The world hangs on a thread, and that thread is the psyche of man." It is my hope that the reader of this text will gain a better grasp of their psyche so that the thread Jung warned us about can become a steel synapse. The task before each of us is to look into deeply held beliefs and convictions to see if we can align what we perceive with what we need to realize. This will allow us to think with clarity and a reasoned purpose that portrays a productive focus on the future.

1

FOUNDATIONS

In any discussion of significant magnitude it is important to set some basic ground rules and give as much background information as possible so that the reader is on the same page as the writer. It is important within the broad context of human thought to agree on some basic premises so that progress can be made in guiding the reader in order to make the intellectual connections that are the motivating force behind this text. With that in mind let us proceed.

Mankind is filled with examples of an inexplicable binary nature. The human form is symmetrical, cut us in half and you will have two almost exact pieces. Man tends to see things as good or evil, black or white, even or odd, win or lose, right or wrong, and left or right just to name a few. The most basic reason for the phenomena probably stems from the concept of balance. The Earth is a sphere, cut it in half anywhere and you get two equal halves. Two symmetrical legs allow us to walk. Every action has an equal and opposite reaction. The two hemispheres of our brain allow for balance in acquiring information, storing that information and using that information in a way that makes sense. Even though there may be three, four or even five sides to an issue, man tends to narrow down their perception into two polar opposites.

Pythagoras said: "If there be light, then there is darkness; if cold, heat; if height, depth; if solid, fluid; if hard, soft; if rough, smooth; if calm, tempest; if prosperity, adversity; if life, death." Following this premise it is not difficult to see how man has binary worldviews. It is not a stretch to accept the supposition that man tends to see problems from two perspectives. One can safely speculate that man has two different visions of how the world operates and tends to divide all aspects of social debate and cognitive perspective into two distinct camps.

When we see the world from one of two different perspectives we apply a linear understanding to the social structures and institutions in which we live. This in itself would be fine if one truly understood why they react and how they apply their perceptions to the social fabric on a daily basis. The problem lies when we apply linear visions to the society in a random way. For instance, why is it that some see the Columbine tragedy resulting from a lack of government control over handguns while others point to the breakdown of family, educational, and religious discipline? The arguments used to explain teen violence lead to linear solutions that affect the social fabric in ways that are not always productive because articulating the factual cause of a social problem is not an easy process. In fact, many of the solutions offered by politicians and social activists only make matters worse. Clearly, blind solutions based on blind perceptions have no place in a modern and literate civilization.

Unfortunately, most of us do not truly understand why we think the way we do and react to the world with a vision which is so closely guarded. We accept and believe our worldviews without question and apply them as if they are the only correct set of mental understandings. Our worldviews are a result of many factors that have worked together to build a cognitive mental model of the world and its innermost workings. Worldviews are so deeply rooted that people will die for their vision yet they can't articulate what their worldview stands for or where it comes from.

Terry Eagleton underscored the depth of passion one subscribes to their worldview:

> What persuades men and women to mistake each other from time to time for gods or vermin is ideology. One can understand well enough how human beings may struggle and murder for good material reasons— reasons connected, for instance, with their physical survival. It is much harder to grasp how they may come to do so in the name of something as apparently abstract as ideas. Yet ideas are what men and women live by, and will occasionally die for.

What makes some people view the world in one way while another set of people see the world in a completely opposite way? In the chapters that follow several specific areas will be discussed that act to define the sequence of events and attitudes that are formed as one develops. The fundamental concepts that are identified during the personal growth process include morality, needs, learning, power, leadership, theology, human nature and nature. Together they play a powerful role in shaping an individual worldview. The perception that defines these concepts will take some in the direction of one worldview and others in a completely opposite direction. That would be fine if for one problem; the worldview one possesses is dangerous if it is defined by blind perceptions. This danger will be detailed in part III of the text as we look to apply the two perceptual views to each of the five social institutions that act as cornerstones of a civilized society.

The journey to define one's worldview is an important one. Each worldview believes in the concepts that will be outlined in the next few chapters but each will apply these concepts in differing ways. It will become obvious very quickly which worldview you subscribe to. All you will need to do is align your perceptions of how the world works in relation to the concept being discussed.

What is a worldview? A worldview or vision is a mental image or the ability to see or perceive something through mental acuteness. An individual perception is based on two processes, interpretation of incoming data and expectancy or how we project our thoughts forward in an outward direction onto the world in which we interact. As a result, the cognitive developmental processes that constructs a perception of the world are influenced by an individuals cognitive ability, acuteness, interpretation and expectancy based on the interplay of nature and nurture. In short, an individual worldview develops based on perceptual growth that can change in depth and accuracy over time. The perceptual reality one currently functions under is represented by either of two historic visions that describe the world around us. Many have discussed the differing perceptions that make up our binary worldviews and a careful examination to these definitions will serve to begin our understanding of these two unique perceptions of the world.

For discussion in this book we will call the two worldviews that underscore mans existence "Universal/Natural" and "Humanistic/Synthetic". The reason the perceptions will be given two words to describe them stems from the fact that man tends to view theories given single names with blinders on, ascribing predetermined connotations to the particular word being used. Like a horse that is easily distracted, man would rather not have to be bothered by something so troublesome as critical thought. As a result, confusion and cognitive apathy inhibits the creation of new paradigms or mental models and constructs. Although an individual may have the talents of a triple-crown winner, blind perceptions only offer success in limited arenas. If we are to begin to evaluate and understand the perceptual models that we associate with our worldview, it is imperative that we begin the journey without interference from previous definitions and the associated biases that have been ascribed theretofore.

Let us look at the definitions of the words that will be used to symbolize the discussion of our binary worldviews with help from Webster's New World Dictionary.

> *Universal:* Of the universe or the totality of all things that exist; present everywhere. Connotation: Pertaining to the dynamic of man and the earth in relationship to the vastness of all that is unexplained.

> *Natural:* Of or dealing with nature; produced or existing in nature; not artificial. Connotation: Pertaining to man's relationship to the world that is guided by laws that are beyond man's grasp.

> *Humanistic:* Any system of thought based on the interests and ideals of man. Connotation: Pertaining to man's belief that he can control his environment and create improvement based on what he believes to be possible.

> *Synthetic:* Not real; artificial. The combining of parts or elements so as to form a whole. Connotation: Pertaining to man's belief that he can formulate an environment outside a natural order.

The term Universal/Natural describes a worldview in which the society is greater than the individual. It will be used to understand behavior that believes the means justify the end. It is a vision of rational pessimism tempered by a belief that man has limited potential yet equal capacity. In the context of modern verbiage the term Universal/Natural most resembles the doctrine of modern conservatism and in some respects that of modern Republicans. Thomas Sowell called the Universal/Natural view "Constrained", while Steven Pinker called it the "Tragic vision".

Martin Luther King, Jr. summed up the Universal/Natural worldview in respect to means and ends when he said: "Immoral means cannot bring moral ends, for the ends are preexistent in the means."

The term Humanistic/Synthetic describes a worldview that sees the individual as greater than the society. It will be used to describe behavior that believes the ends justify the means. It is a vision of blind optimism of what man can create sustained by a belief in man's unlimited potential and superiority by the few to guide the less capable masses. In the context of modern verbiage the term Humanistic/Synthetic most resembles modern liberalism or Progressivism and in some respects the dogma of modern Democrats. Thomas Sowell called the Humanistic/Synthetic view the "Unconstrained" or "Vision of the Anointed", while Stephen Pinker described it as the "Utopian vision".

The Humanistic/Synthetic worldview's utopian overtones underscore the basic premise of the vision where beliefs in ideas such as engineering world peace are commonplace. James Madison offered some thoughts as to the validity of such ideas: "A universal peace, it is to be feared, is in the catalog of events, which will never exist but in the imaginations of visionary philosophers, or in the breasts of benevolent enthusiasts."

George F. Will defined the two worldviews in terms of optimism and pessimism. The Universal/Natural vision in this definition is idealistically pessimistic, while the Humanistic/Synthetic vision could be one of optimistic idealism:

> One of the pleasures of being a conservative is that you are always more or less pleased. Conservatives are pessimists, so when things go badly they have the pleasure of having their beliefs confirmed, and when they go well they enjoy the pleasant surprise.

This is not to be confused with saying someone who is a Universal/Natural thinker is a modern Republican or a Humanistic/Synthetic thinker is a modern Democrat. Even though there are some similarities, the confusion of easily defining packages of thought will lead the reader to misrepresent themselves and miss the opportunity to truly define what worldview they actually ascribe. It is important to remember that words are just a method of communicating and one must not fall into the trap of assuming meaning quickly and then inserting all sorts of predetermined definitions into the discussion. Individuals can call themselves anything they like or associate to whatever political organization they so choose. How one perceives the world however may in fact be far different than the doctrine of a particular social structure one aligns with.

The terms chosen have partial significance in describing a particular worldview from its namesake. It is vital however that the reader does not get caught up in the words and miss the understanding of the underlying theory that is being conveyed in this text. If each individual applies old definitions and assumptions about the meaning of words, confusion will undermine their ability to have clarity of thought. Political leaders of both world views have done a masterful job of disguising their true ideology by using words to deceive followers into believing they champion a principle when, in fact, the actions of the leadership is counter to the very principle they claim to represent. In other words, be careful.

John Locke spoke of the confusion words can create:

> Vague and mysterious forms of speech, and abuse of language, have so long passed for mysteries of science; and hard or misapplied words with little or no meaning have, by prescription, such a right to be mistaken for deep learning and height of speculation, that it will not be easy to persuade either those who speak or those who hear them, that they are covers of ignorance and hindrance of true knowledge.

To explain how confusing words have made the understanding of complex processes, lets look at some examples of words that have been used to trick or deceive. The Federalists of early America named those who were against them Anti-Federalists when in fact the Anti-Federalists were the ones who most believed in Federalism. The term liberal today describes a dogma that is the opposite of its earlier use when liberalism conveyed a perspective that was against the status quo of governmental control through the monarchy or religious domination by an all-powerful Catholic Church. In both of these examples the institutions held more power than the individual and it was the liberal philosophy that aimed its beliefs against those powerful forces.

James Q. Wilson also points out how the definitions of the words liberal and conservative have changed:

> In early 19th century a liberal was a person who favored personal and economic liberty; that is freedom from the control and power of the state. A conservative was originally a person who opposed the excesses of the French Revolution and its emphasis on personal freedom and favored instead a restoration of the power of the state, the church and the aristocracy.

Classical liberalism today is called modern conservatism and what was once thought of as conservatism is now the doctrine of modern liberal ideology. With that said, it could just as easily be shown that current Democrats and Republicans who serve in a political sense fall into the same worldview, that of being Humanistic/Synthetic. This in itself is a interesting and daunting concept but the analysis of the current confusion among our most powerful leaders will be left for another time.

It is no wonder that we are perplexed when it comes to understanding just what defines our worldview. To fully begin to determine the worldview one holds, it will be necessary to compare and test numerous examples and perspectives against one's unique mental framework of the world. This analysis will show a definitive tendency as to which way one sees the world and its operation.

In the discussion of the two worldviews it is important to note that the text builds upon a theoretical model based on the assumption that man is either in one school of thought or the other. For descriptive clarity and purpose, consistency to the worldview is assumed. However, it needs to be noted that there are gray areas that are produced when one is moving between one worldview and towards another or when intellectual inconsistencies align conflicting perceptions. Even though there are differences in individuals as well as varying developmental rates, a worldview will develop for most that has a strong tendency but will not be totally aligned with one side or the other.

An important theory of this text will be to show that many individuals will move from a Humanistic/Synthetic to a Universal/Natural worldview as they get older or grow in a developmental sense. The famous Winston Churchill quote offers the theory of worldviews that develop and change some credibility: "Any 20 year-old who isn't a liberal doesn't have a heart, and any 40 year-old who isn't a conservative doesn't have a brain."

For each of us, our worldview begins to develop at birth and continues to expand as we acquire a greater understanding of the world. At some time for most of us, the world is perceived from the Humanistic/Synthetic perspective. For many, our worldview will continue to develop until it is transformed into the Universal/Natural vision. This process evolves in proportion to the amount of individual cognitive effort, understanding and acceptance of truths one is willing to assimilate. Steven Pinker notes that: "liberal and conservative attitudes are heritable not, of course, because attitudes are synthesized directly from DNA but because they come naturally to people with different temperaments." Thus, an individual's DNA plays a role in determining ones worldview by offering unique tendencies of personality traits. When this is coupled to influential environmental factors, an individual's worldview is solidified.

The state of cognitive awareness an individual possesses at any point in time, as far as their worldview goes, may be in transition and show a great deal of intellectual inconsistency. The transitional nature of worldviews further muddies the waters of defining and articulating one's specific perception of the world. With that said however, it is not impossible to associate and connect one's current worldview with the two visions that will be discussed.

Ian Anderson summed up his interpretation of the two worldviews by offering an analogy. He said that the Universal/Natural see the world as if it were a sea, controlled by natural laws where the creatures that inhabit it are free to do as they wish with the good and bad of nature as a backdrop. In contrast, the Humanistic/Synthetic see the world as a fish bowl that is controlled by external surrogate decision makers that determine the level of health and freedom of the fish and their environment through an engineered approach.

Thomas Jefferson described the two worldviews in a letter he wrote in 1825:

> Men by their constitutions are naturally divided into two parties: (1) Those who fear and distrust the people, and wish to draw all powers from them into the hands of the higher classes. (2) Those who identify themselves with the people, have confidence in them, cherish and consider them as the most honest and safe, although not the most wise depository of the public interests. In every country these parties exist; and in every one where they are free to think, speak, and write, they will declare themselves.

Group (1) according to Jefferson would be characterized as having a Humanistic/Synthetic worldview while (2) would see the world from a Universal/Natural mind set. It may seem at face value that the opposite is true but as we define the underlying perceptions of each vision one will see the clarity of Jefferson's words. Ironically, the modern Democratic Party holds Jefferson as its founder when in fact Jefferson's worldview is more closely aligned with that of the Universal/Natural perspective. The left can connect to Jefferson in this way because most if not all of the founders saw the world through the lens of the Universal/Natural vision which was counter to the powerful control of the English crown. Thus, there is a theoretical connection from both modern worldviews in America to the roots of the founder's beliefs.

Malcolm Muggeridge described one worldview as liberal humanism. He defines the Humanistic/Synthetic worldview in which man feels he has the capacity to engineer and create a utopian world without the burdens of natural law:

> Where no creature in the universe is greater than man. Where the future of the human race rests only with human beings themselves, which leads infallibly to some sort of suicidal situation. The efforts of men in this vision to bring about their own happiness, their own self-indulgence, will in due course produce the opposite.

The Humanistic/Synthetic mind set can also be known as a worldview called Statism. In this vision, regulation and control of individual behavior comes from elite governmental surrogate decision-makers and pioneers of modern politically correct behavior and thought. The problem with this vision is that unbridled political correctness can produce social structures like we saw in Germany in the 1940's under Hitler. Remember, what Hitler was saying was politically correct in Germany and blindly perceived as an accurate set of social assumptions. It goes unsaid that the outcome of Germans' blindly following the mindless political correctness Hitler exposed was a scar on all of humanity.

Today, unchecked political correctness in America is becoming the cultural Zeitgeist or trend of thought. So damaging is the modern PC culture that Dennis Miller once remarked that he "was afraid to separate his laundry for fear of being called a racist." All joking aside, campus speech codes, sensitivity training, multiculturalism, values clarification, and a host of other "appropriate" modes of "proper thinking and behaving" have become the common secular religion of today. The culture war America now faces is creating the polarization of what was once known as the "melting pot" and turning it into a politically correct "salad bowl". Unfortunately, the cultural balkanization of America will not bring us together as is hoped by those with blind perceptions; instead it will ultimately create the type of bloody divisiveness we have seen in places like Eastern Europe and Africa. Remembering the Rhwanda genocide of 1994 that killed 500,000–800,000 in the span of 100 days provides a sobering example of the effects that human nature coupled to balkanized nations can manifest.

The modern liberal theory of the Humanistic/Synthetic worldview has also been called Reductionism. In this description, the view of the world is defined by a realism of people who are blind to reality. Thus, what is seen as true or objective is refracted through a cognitive lens that is incapable of clarity or the ability to perceive the world without misrepresentation. In other words, they live within a cognitive framework of blind perceptions.

This text will define the worldviews not only in a narrative form but by also adding visual mental models. This will allow the reader to see the two worldviews side by side allowing for comparison and contrast in a visual medium. Hopefully this will provide a user-friendly format to differentiate and contemplate each worldview.

For the purposes of visual understanding into the opposing worldviews, graphic descriptions will be given with the Humanistic/Synthetic worldview on the left and the Universal/Natural vision presented on the right. These descriptions do follow the modern understanding of what one would call the left and the right in a political sense but one must caution against prejudging the descriptions without examining the concepts associated with each side.

Now that we have established some basic assumptions concerning man's binary nature, the next step is to explore the development process that builds our worldview. Before that analysis is undertaken, we must outline the ramifications of acting upon blind perceptions in order to underscore the importance of undertaking the personal growth process and assimilate a more appropriate set of worldview standards.

Foundations

Humanistic/Synthetic	Universal/Natural
Left	Right
Individual greater than society	Society greater than individual
Ends justify the means	Means justify the ends
Optimistic idealism	Rational Pessimism
Unlimited potential/unequal capacity	Limited potential/equal capacity
Superiority of the few	Natural law
Engineered utopia	Tragic vision
Blind perceptions	Constrained vision
Unconstrained vision	
Utopian vision	
Vision of the anointed	
Political correctness	

2

WORLDVIEWS AND THE DECLINE OF MODERN CIVILIZATION

Now that we have defined the two opposing worldviews we must turn our attention towards understanding the impact each has on civilization. Chapters 3 through 10 will examine the specific concepts that act upon the developmental process of shaping worldviews. Chapters 10 through 16 will apply the worldviews to the institutions of civilized society. Chapter 2 will outline the necessity to understand one's vision of the world so the institutions holding us together can be maintained.

Every individual perceives civilization through a worldview that guides their decisions on a myriad of topics. They do so by applying their vision to the social institutions that act as pillars holding our civilization together. The five institutions that are the glue to the maintenance of civilized society are Government, Economics, Education, Family and Religion. Each of these institutions plays a vital role in shaping the fundamental health of our society by allowing the social fabric to function in a manner that maintains the health of modern life. Institutions do so because each offers behavioral constraints so that man can function within a civilized society. Unfortunately, these pillars are susceptible to damage or outright collapse.

The worldviews that are at odds have been seen for as long as man has been keeping records. The two visions at best act as opposing forces holding the civilization together. At worst, binary visions create a situation that undermines the very foundations necessary for our survival. It is for this very reason that we must understand the dynamic interplay between the necessary social institutions and the two visions that dominate our culture. To do this one must first comprehend why one thinks as they do and then look to see how that thinking, when applied to the interaction with institutions, causes harmony in society or tears at the very fabric one assumes they are helping to strengthen. It is our intellectual inconsistencies that create problems and if we, as a society, do not begin the mental journey in aligning what we think with what we do, we will destroy ourselves without the knowledge that it has even happened until it is too late.

To exemplify this concept we can look to the analogy of a story that has been told by Leonard Reed. It is not important if the science of the story is true or not. What is critical is the understanding of how we can be destroying our civilization without even the slightest inkling that we are caught up in the process.

The analogy is called the frog in the pot and it goes something like this. If one places a pot of water on the stove, brings the temperature to a boil and then throws a frog into the boiling water, the frog will jump out of the pot as quickly as you can say hot. The frog understands and quickly reacts to the environmental stimulus in order to avoid the consequences, namely being cooked. However, if a pot of water at room temperature is placed on the stove and a frog is placed in the water it will not jump out because the environment is not seen as dangerous. If the water temperature is then slowly brought to a boil the frog will not perceive the environmental danger. The slowly rising temperature will go undetected by the frog until it is too late and the frog is too weak to save itself. The result will be that the frog will cook itself to death even though the frog had the capacity to easily save itself.

The health of our civilization works in much the same way. The question that begs to be asked is will we perceive the changes that are occurring to our social institutions and adjust our behavior accordingly or will we, like the frog, be lulled into complacency by the slow changes that are taking place within our environment? The answer lies in realization of our worldviews and the behavior they manifest. If we do not approach civilization with a clear and definitive set of appropriate assumptions we will create conditions that cause the collapse of our institutions. Even if we do realize that there are serious problems in our environment will it be too late to save ourselves from destruction?

It is important to take notice of and adjust the developmental patterns of views that work for and against our cultural institutions. This will provide for a balance of visions that will create a "best case" scenario. One of the troubling aspects is thinking society is in a state of balance within a left/right worldview continuum because we recognize both visions at play. Society must guard itself in believing that balance is being achieved just because we think we see two visions counteracting each other when in reality what we may be seeing is only the two extremes of one world view. In short, will we detect environmental changes or not?

Throughout time, many great civilizations have come and gone. Ancient history reminds us that the great Roman Empire is no more, while modern history is forever engraved with the failure of the Soviet Union. Victor Davis Hansen has detailed and explained the Roman analogy we so often hear today:

> Earlier Romans knew what it was to be Roman, why it was at least better than the alternative, and why the culture had to be defended. Later, in ignorance, they forgot what they knew, in pride mocked who they were, and, in consequence, disappeared.

Maybe we will pay the same price those before us faced or, with a little foresight, maybe we can avoid the mistakes others have blindly miscalculated. It is ironic that The United States was founded upon the failures of the British Empire and yet it seems as if we are creating a culture that is practicing many of those same mistakes. If we have the intellectual capital to truly unlock the pitfalls that have ravaged others we can move our civilization forward in concert with our place in destiny.

To exemplify this situation, many great thinkers have pondered the question concerning binary worldviews and maintenance of civilization. Lets take a look at what they had to say that may offer insight into how we can help make our civilization flourish.

Friedrich A. Hayek clearly articulated the current situation of conflicting worldviews:

> The fundamental situation man is faced with is found within the interplay between the two visions. These two unique perspectives of how the world works are at odds with each other. The vision of human limits (Universal/Natural) offers a best case view while the vision of ever expanding human capacity (Humanistic/Synthetic) pushes civilization in a direction that will ultimately create a scenario of human decline.

It is important to note once again that great civilizations have come and gone throughout the course of human history and it would be ignorant of us to not look at these historical representations of human failure and not learn from their mistakes. Unfortunately the vision of unending human capacity blinds itself, by its very nature, to knowledge that is readily available to ana-lyze.

Hayek continues by saying:

> The reason one vision will destroy civilization as we know it and have grown accustomed to is in its most basic sense is the inability to see mans inherent limits. The humanistic (Synthetic) vision blindly believes man can alter forces more powerful than they can comprehend. The ability of man to reason without limits is in of itself its fatal error in reasoning and thus its downfall. Unfortunately the humanistic (Synthetic) vision is blind to this and forges ahead without fear or malice.

For instance, the call for universal health care in the 1990's seems at face value to be reasonable and yet the methodology and institutional realignment necessary to create such a system would create irreparable damage to the very fabric that holds our civilization together. Fortunately, this political wolf did not come to fruition, but the core belief system lies just under the surface and will soon reappear in sheep's clothes.

Hayek cautions us by offering a sobering conclusion and shows why the society needs to be placed in context ahead of the individual:

> It may indeed prove to be far the most difficult and not the least impor-tant task for human reason rationally to comprehend its own limitations. It is essential for the growth of reason that as individuals we should bow to forces and obey principles which we cannot hope fully to understand, yet on which the advance and even the preservation of civilization depend.

In other words there is no "I" in team. The irony is that the Humanistic/ Synthetic utilize a worldview that places man at the center to produce a win-ning civilization. Unfortunately, a game plan based on this blind assumption will lose big to a team called "universality". What may be far more ironically humorous or scary, depending on your interpretation; is that our institutions of higher learning that promote the Humanistic/Synthetic vision are called universities.

In shaping the necessary understanding of the interplay of the two world-views that are vital to the advancement of our civilization Hayek articulates the confusion between the two worldviews. "It is largely because civilization enables us constantly to profit from knowledge which we individually do not possess and because each individual's use of his particular knowledge may serve to assist others unknown to him in achieving their ends that men as members of civilized society can pursue their individual ends so much more successfully than they could alone." In other words, the collective knowledge of individuals to effect systemic change trumps the elite knowledge of a few in advancing society.

To Hayek, lacking a belief in something greater than self is the fatal error in reasoning within the Humanistic/Synthetic vision. In contrast, the Universal/Natural vision understands the limits of man's place in a dynamic universe. They view the best case civilization for man as one in which institutions are set up by social contract allowing society to live within the institutional framework in order to economize knowledge. This produces the best society possible, mindful of limits and faithful in the order of a universe far beyond our ability to comprehend its make up. The Universal/Natural vision understands that knowledge articulated through the behavior of the masses will far exceed any knowledge accumulated by individuals or small groups of elite decision-makers. Sadly, the social contract system that governs productive and successful civilizations is quickly being replaced with a system of individual contracts made between man and himself without regard to others.

Today's sophists believe they can work within a vacuum outside the universal order while prudent pragmatists fear the explosion a vacuum unleashes upon its violation.

In short, man can create all sorts of utopias in the mind but in the end we will be pitting ourselves against an order in which we do not even have the most basic understanding. It is this futile belief in those with the Humanistic/Synthetic vision that we are capable of ruling and overcoming forces beyond the limits of man that will destroy any chance for sustaining our precarious existence in a form we are accustomed to.

It is this contradictory continuum that creates confusion among men and their perceptions of how to best apply their worldview to society. Although we must work from a standpoint of individual decisions to create the best possible society, the individual alone, void of a universal frame of reference, will build institutions that will not be able to hold up under the weight of man's limited place in a dynamic universe. Thus it is paramount that we come to terms with the theoretical perceptions that are at odds, and merge them into a model that will allow us to move forward and not towards our demise with blind impunity.

Kenneth Clark was more pragmatic than philosophical in dealing with the necessary institutions of civilization: "The dreary fact remains, that, even in the darkest ages, it was institutions that made society work, and if civilization is to survive, society must somehow be made to work."

John Buchan was far more pessimistic when he discussed the tenuous nature of our civilization: "You think that a wall as solid as the earth separates civilization from barbarism. I tell you the division is a thread, a sheet of glass. A touch here, a push there, and you bring back the reign of Saturn."

Hayek offered wisdom when he stated that "The ultimate decision about what is accepted as right and wrong will be made not by individual human wisdom but by the disappearance of the groups that have adhered to the wrong beliefs." The problem is, the Humanistic/Synthetic worldview is becoming dominant in our culture and thus the group that will disappear that Hayek speaks of will be the total of our modern society.

Lastly, Albert Einstein cautioned us to a sobering reality: "We shall require a substantially new manner of thinking if mankind is to survive."

A graphic representation is presented to help illustrate the terms used to describe the two worldviews. Note that the Humanistic/Synthetic worldview has far more terminology or schools of thought than the worldview of the Universal/Natural. The cause of this may be related to the developmental level of the Humanistic/Synthetic mind that finds itself confused when trying to explain what they perceive. As a result, the Humanistic/Synthetic feel a need to reinvent their philosophical foundations to create fresh, but not necessarily new, definitions to explain and legitimize their worldview.

Many align themselves to these representative terms and yet their worldview is inconsistent with the principles that guide a particular school of thought. Because of the numerous terms used to describe a specific worldview, it is obvious that confusion and inconsistencies will occur. Thus, it is highly important in this discussion to see beyond trendy nomenclature and understand the primary features each worldview is based upon.

Clearly the maintenance of civilization hangs in the balance between behavior that sustains our existence and that which destroys society slowly from within. To avoid the collapse of our civilization, the next step is to undertake the study into the mechanisms of worldview development.

World Views and the Decline of Modern Civilization

Humanistic/Synthetic	Universal/Natural
Liberal Humanism	Classical Liberalism
Secular Humanism	Ideological Republicans
Modern Liberalism	Vision of human limits
Classical Conservatism	Modern Conservatism
Progressives	
Ideological Democrats	
Democratic Socialists	
Moral Relativists	
Reductionists	
Statists	
Materialism	
Vision of ever expanding human capacity	
Man can control nature	
Reason without limits	

II

WORLDVIEW
DEVELOPMENT

Now that we have established that the two world visions guide our social perspective and decision making in a way that is vital to the advancement of civilization; it is time to answer the question as to how worldviews develop within individuals. In other words, where do our distinct visions come from and how are they formed?

Part II of this text will examine several areas that impact the human developmental process. The following chapters will discuss morality, needs, learning, power, leadership, theology, human nature, and nature. These areas of human cognitive growth play a pivotal role in the direction that guide each of us toward one of the worldviews. The chapters that follow will also correlate how one's worldview can be transformed over time as further cognitive development takes place.

By connecting the diverse fields and underlying theories within the social sciences as they apply to the building of individual worldviews a road map will be produced to guide the reader to self-awareness. This will allow us to recognize why we perceive the world from the perspective of the Universal/Natural vision or the Humanistic/Synthetic vision. Hopefully this will allow for productive decision-making based on reasoned thought instead of harmful suppositions based on blind perceptions.

3

MORALITY

"Civilization depends on morality."—Ralph Waldo Emerson

The first concept that acts as a developer of our worldview surrounds the formation of morality and values within the individual. In order to understand how each of us defines morality and applies that perspective to a worldview, the theories of Lawrence Kolberg must be given a thoughtful visit.

In 1971, Lawrence Kolberg developed a theory of moral development that paralleled the developmental stages of other pioneers in psychology. In a nutshell, Kolberg showed how human cognitive developmental processes play a role in the sequence and scope of moral understanding. Kolberg connected the developmental processes into three stages: Pre-conventional morality, Conventional morality and Post-conventional morality.

Pre-conventional morality is the defining of right and wrong based on the potential use of force. Conventional morality is the defining of right and wrong based on the need to feel acceptance by the group. Post-conventional morality is the defining of right and wrong based on the ability to stand on principles, values and traditions regardless of the threat of force or acceptance from a group. Post-conventional morality also shows the cognitive ability to grasp the concepts of social contracts and universal moral truths within its theoretical framework.

The person who works from a Post-conventional moral position is fully aware of the importance of the concept of social contracts. In a system of social contracts institutions of civilization are created by men who then live within a contractual agreement with those institutions in order to survive.

Additionally, one who has attained Post-conventional morality understands and accepts that there are universal moral truths that transcend and are beyond the scope of human institutions. In other words, what is right and wrong in a moral sense comes from a higher order or power that is beyond the scope and understanding of mans limited ability to alter the dynamics of the universe. Thus, the Post-conventional man understands both the social contracts of institutional living as well as the laws that transcend the institutions are at play.

For example, the unalienable rights to life, liberty and happiness or property outlined in the Declaration of Independence are based on moral truths that define what is right within the context of universal principles or laws that relate to man. The right to life deals with universals of social/cultural freedom within the kingdom of man including but not limited to religion, education and family. The right to liberty deals with universals of political and governmental freedom. Lastly, the right to property deals with universals of economic freedom. These universal moral truths transcend human law and understanding. Of course man has the capacity to circumvent these universal laws by institutional controls, but to do so is counter to the natural order. In short, the Post-conventional man accepts the fact that there are natural laws/moral truths that guide the universe.

Universal natural laws are as fundamental as the natural laws found in science and they apply to all animals that live within social structures, For example, a pod of dolphins also live within the context of the concepts of life, liberty, and happiness or property as previously mentioned. They do so because these universal functions are absolute. The "right" to life for the dolphins means that they are free to develop social structures of family and education to ensure the survival of the young. The "right" to liberty for the dolphins means that they are free to form governmental structures through the creation of social rules and a hierarchy of authority. Lastly, the "right" to property for the dolphins means that they function in ways that answer the economic questions of what, how and for whom as they relate to a life of unlimited wants in an under sea world of limited resources.

The stages of moral development are bracketed around age groups. Kolberg said that the Pre-conventional level was in use between 0 and 6 years of age, while Conventional morality was achieved between 7-11 years of age and Post-conventional morality was attained after 11 years of age. One must not assume however that all people go through these stages of morality at these approximate time frames. Growing up developmentally past the conventional stage of morality may in fact be the fundamental difference between the Humanistic/Synthetic mind and that of the Universal/Natural. In essence, when one fully grows up developmentally they attain Post-conventional morality and a Universal/Natural worldview.

As an essential part of our development process the attainment of these stages or the lack therein impacts our worldviews. Better yet, the worldview one will apply to their social setting either consciously or not is determined to some degree by one's level of moral development. The Humanistic/Synthetic worldview shows a Pre-conventional or Conventional level of morality while the Universal/Natural world view is based on a Conventional or Post-conventional understanding of the world.

To help us define how moral development influences our worldviews let us use Lawrence Kolberg's own words to describe the perception and application of thought from the Pre-conventional or Conventional morality that permeates the Humanistic/Synthetic world view. We can then look to the opposite perceptions and application of thought as we apply the theory of Post-conventional morality to the Universal/Natural worldview.

Stages of Moral Development by Lawrence Kohlberg (1971)

I. *Pre-conventional Level*
At this level, the child is responsive to cultural rules and labels of good and bad, right or wrong, but he interprets the labels in terms of either the physical or hedonistic consequences of action (punishment, reward, exchange of favors) or the physical power of those who enunciate the rules and labels. The level is divided into the following three stages.

Stage 0: Egocentric judgment. The child makes judgments of good on the basis of what he likes and wants or what helps him, and bad on the basis of what he does not like or what hurts him. He has no concept of rules or of obligations to obey or conform independent of his wish.

Stage 1: The punishment and obedience orientation. The physical consequences of action determine its goodness or badness regardless of the human meaning or value of these consequences. Avoidance of punishment and unquestioning deference to power are values in their own right, not in terms of respect for an underlying moral order supported by punishment and authority (the latter is stage 4).

Stage 2: The instrumental relativist orientation. Right action consists of what instrumentally satisfies one's own needs and occasionally the needs of others. Human relations are viewed in terms such as those of the market place. Elements of fairness, reciprocity, and equal sharing are present, but they are always interpreted in a physical, pragmatic way. Reciprocity is a matter of "you scratch my back and I'll scratch your", not loyalty, gratitude, or justice.

II. *Conventional Level*:
At this level, the individual perceives the maintenance of the expectations of his family, group, or nation as valuable in its own right, regardless of immediate and obvious consequences. The attitude is not only one of conformity to personal expectations and social order, but of loyalty to it, of actively maintaining, supporting, and justifying the order and identifying with the persons or group involved in it. The level consists of the following two stages:

Stage 3: The interpersonal concordance or "good boy-nice girl" orientation. Good behavior is what pleases or helps others and is approved by them. There is much conformity to stereotypical images of what is majority or "natural" behavior. Behavior is frequently judged by intention—"he means well" becomes important for the first time. One earns approval by being "nice".

Stage 4: The "law and order" orientation. The individual is oriented toward authority, fixed rules, and the maintenance of the social order. Right behavior consists in doing one's duty, showing respect for authority, and maintaining the given social order for its own sake.

III. *Post-Conventional, Autonomous, or Principled Level.*
The individual makes a clear effort to define moral values and principles that have validity and application apart from the authority of the groups of persons holding them and apart from the individual's own identification with the group. The level has the two following stages:

Stage 5: The social-contract legalistic orientation (generally with utilitarian overtones). Right action tends to be defined in terms of general individual rights and standards that have been critically examined and agreed upon by the whole society. There is a clear awareness of the relativism of personal values and opinions and a corresponding emphasis upon procedural rules for reaching consensus. Aside from what is constitutionally and democratically agreed upon, right action is a matter of personal values and opinions. The result is an emphasis upon the "legal point of view", but with an additional emphasis upon the possibility of changing the law in terms of rational considerations of social utility (rather than freezing it in terms of stage 4 "law and order"). Outside the legal realm, free agreement, and contract, is the binding element of obligation. The "official" morality of the American government and Constitution is at this stage.

Stage 6: The universal ethical-principle orientation. Right is defined by the decision of conscience in accord with self-chosen ethical principles that appeal to logical comprehensiveness, universality, and consistency. These principles are abstract and ethical (the Golden Rule, the categorical imperative); they are not concrete moral rules like the Ten Command-ments. At heart, these are universal principles of justice, of the reciprocity and equality of the human rights, and of respect for the dignity of human beings as individual persons.

Kolberg clearly underscores the importance that moral development has in defining one's world perspective. It is important to note that the timing ques-tion is vital to understanding how individuals can assume one moral perspec-tive and thus one particular worldview for many years of their life and then later, because of further cognitive growth, acquire the opposite vision. As Churchill's famous quote summarizes; the young are emotional and liberal, while the old are more reasoned and conservative. It is obvious however that some will never achieve the cognitive moral ability to move past even the Pre-conventional level. This is due to the fact that genetic or environmental influ-ences have created an operational structure within the brain that inhibits the cognitive processes needed to perceive the world beyond a limited capacity. For example, an abused or overly pampered child may develop a cognitive map that is influenced so strongly as the result of the abuse, or lack of accountabil-ity, that they are never fully able to perceive the world from a Post-conven-tional frame of reference.

In short, the morality of the Humanistic/Synthetic is tied to the individual while the morality of the Universal/Natural is tied to the greater society. C. Evans said:

Attainment of the Post-Conventional level requires a student to move past viewing laws as right and believing in one's own obligation to fulfilling a social contract. When giving full consideration to each member's perspective of a moral situation, decisions are based on an ethic of responsibility to society.

There is a gray area when advancing from one stage of moral development to another. Do not be confused however by someone who holds a Humanistic/Synthetic worldview that acts or believes they are articulating their vision from the Post-conventional level. Misinterpreting the theory to suit your perceptions is counter to true Post-conventional behavior. Thinking you are at a Post-conventional moral level does not mean your actions are consistent with the principles of that level. Additionally, not everyone with the Universal/Natural worldview has attained Post Conventional morality in practice. What one looks for to see if they are at a Post-conventional level is consistency of words and deeds associated to the proper understanding of the theory that Kohlberg set forth.

In *The Blank Slate*, Steven Pinker discusses Kohlberg's Post Conventional level but connects it to what he calls the Utopian vision (Humanistic/Synthetic). "The utopian vision stresses social responsibility, where people hold their actions to a higher ethical standard…a willingness to ignore rules in favor of abstract principles was literally identified as a higher stage." Pinker suggests that the Humanistic/Synthetic vision is the world view of Post Conventional morality but Kohlberg's theory specifically details in stages 5 and 6 the need to have a social-contract legalistic orientation where self-chosen ethical principles appeal to logical comprehensiveness, universality, and consistency. Clearly Post-conventional morality is not just about ignoring rules in favor of moral equivalency or any abstract principle one might deem appropriate. Achieving Post Conventional morality is most closely related to the Universal/Natural worldview. The specifics of this analysis will be outlined in greater detail throughout the text.

Maurice Maeterlinck added to this when he detailed how the Humanistic/Synthetic can ignore universal moral truths while at the same time defend and expound morality. "Man is so essentially, so necessarily, a moral being, that when he denies the existence of all morality, that very denial already becomes the foundation of a new morality."

Another way to look at the morality question as it applies to worldviews is to understand the "Can I" versus the "Should I" argument. Those with Preconventional or Conventional morality look at problems, issues, worldly questions, etcetera from the stand point of "Can I". If the answer is yes, then the solution is to move forward without application of the "Should I". On the other hand, the Post-conventional moralist when faced with problems, issues, worldly questions, etcetera looks to the "Should I" to offer guidance beyond the selfish interests of human nature. In other words the Humanistic/Synthetic vision answers the "Should I" with yes, because "I can". While the Universal/Natural vision answers the "Should I" with a deference to a higher order as well as institutional incentives asking in effect "Can I" or "May I".

William Pfaff articulated the Humanistic/Synthetic focus on the "Can I" when he stated:

> The West no longer acknowledges the existence of an external rule-giver or moral authority. It regards mankind as entirely autonomous, existing within a moral framework entirely of its own creation, responsible only to itself.

He continues by saying a moral authority has been central to Western beliefs historically. Pfaff argues that a natural law to which men are morally obligated was taken for granted by the Founding Fathers and in fact the concept of natural rights existing outside human institutions was seen as an absolute:

> Today in the Western world there is no general acknowledgement of an external standard or reference for how man should conduct himself. The thoughts that guided the old Western thought have been replaced with secular political and scientific utopias instead of a religious expectation of a salvation located outside of time and history. The current belief is that man is eugenic or can improve his genetic hereditary makeup by a nihilistic practice of changing the existing political and social institutions. By this new view of the world, man is autonomous and has absolute freedom to do whatever he chooses without regard to universal truths or the old Western belief that there are moral laws and rights that transcend man and his behavior.

This lack of deference to a higher power in the West that Pfaff is talking about is commonly called secular humanism or moral relativity. Secular, or non religious humanism, has at its base the notion that theological morality has no place in a perspective that embraces at its core the unique individual and his linear version of how the world works. Moral relativity extends on this fundamental principle for the Humanistic/Synthetic. They believe there are no moral absolutes and that every problem, issue or worldly question can only be answered within the conscience of the individual. This must be allowed without judgment or questioning as to the validity of the assumptions being held.

Victor Davis Hanson offers a sobering example of moral relativity when he states:

> A half century of anthropology, after all, would suggest to us that burqas and clitoridectomies are just "different" or perhaps comparable (or even superior to) Western fashion and custom. Traditional history, on the other hand argues that women across time and space, like men, struggle to be free, not mutilated, and to be treated as equals.

Thomas Jefferson also had some thoughts on morality that is important in the understanding of the narcissism inherent in the Humanistic/Synthetic worldview:

> Self interest, or rather self-love, or egoism, has been more plausibly substituted as the basis of morality. But I consider our relations with others as constituting the boundaries of morality. With ourselves, we stand on the ground of identity, not of relation, which last, requiring two subjects, excludes self love confined to a single one. To ourselves, in strict language, we can owe no duties, obligation requiring also two parties. Self- love, therefore, is no part of morality. Indeed, it is exactly its counterpart.

When looking at the stages of moral development, one must also understand the concept of evil and the role it plays in defining one's moral level. Those who do not accept the fact that there is evil in the world operate at a Pre-conventional or Conventional level of morality in which an external locus of control is given to others and their requisite expectations as to right and wrong. "Group think" mentality is then the methodology used to view the world. This occurs because those who are blind to man's evil potential behave as the result of their inability to accept the evil that is within them. John Locke described this group think/politically correct mode of Conventional morality when he said: "We are like chameleons, we take our hue and the color of our moral character from those around us."

Evil is not accepted because defense mechanisms like repression, denial, displacement, reaction formation, rationalization, projection and sublimation are at play. It is much easier to deny facts than to come to terms with ones self.

The taking of a personal inventory and accepting what nature and nurture has created brings with it a reality that many do not want to face. As a result, mental self-survival tools are in play dictating perception, behavior and moral judgments in lieu of dealing with unresolved personal issues or neurotic over behaviors. If there are no moral absolutes then there is no need to deal with one's self because no judgments will be made.

In other words those in a Pre-conventional or Conventional moral stage need to mature and accept the reality that is a part of their being. For most this happens at some stage in life, but some are forever challenged to see clearly without the fog of personal issues clouding their reality. Sadly, far too many individuals tattoo and pierce their bodies, develop eating disorders, or behave in anti-social ways because the road to self-acceptance and understanding is far tougher than taking the route of outward expressions of inner turmoil.

Quite possibly the most significant difference between the Humanistic/Synthetic and Universal/Natural worldviews is detailed in this discussion of morality and acceptance of self. Those who wish to participate in social movements and undertake social engineering experiments that have no personal cost do so to avoid feelings of inadequacy in order to feel well of themselves. In other words, the vision of the Humanistic/Synthetic allows its subjects the freedom to escape the pain of dealing with inner turmoil through outward expressions of social empathy.

An important example of social engineering movements carried out by the Humanistic/Synthetic worldview is highlighted in the worldwide crusade to ban the pesticide DDT. In the Book "Silent Spring", Rachel Carson discussed what she believed to be the harmful effects of DDT. Her argument was that DDT would wipe out the eggs of birds and destroy many species, with the result being a "silent spring". Although countless advocates of this premise have all but ended the use of DDT with little scientific proof of its effectiveness, the costs to human life has been in the millions as the rise of malaria in developing countries has reached monumental proportions.

The bottom line is that even though social engineers may feel well of themselves and their particular cause in lieu of dealing with personal insignificance, they do not have the right to place enormous costs on the lives of others. This is a clear example of how blind perceptions are harmful to the maintenance of civilization.

In his book: *Between War and Peace,* Victor Davis Hansen outlines the psychology of the social engineers and their limited worldview:

> Such naivete engenders its own array of contradictory attitudes and emotions, including guilt, hypocrisy, and envy. Among some of our new aristocrats, the realization has dawned that their good fortune is not shared worldwide and therefore exists at the expense of others, if not the planet itself. It sends some of them to their fax machines...it prompts others, more principled and more honorable to work in soup kitchens, give money to impoverished school districts, and help out less fortunate friends and family. But local charity is unheralded and also expensive, in terms of both time and money. Far easier for most to exhibit concern by signing an ostentatious petition against Israel or to assemble in Central Park: public demonstrations that cost nothing but seemingly meet the need to show to peers that one is generous, fair, caring, and compassionate.

Thomas Sowell made a similar point in defining the differing worldviews and how the question of morality and evil is perceived and acted upon in the context of social interaction within or between countries:

> In this era of non-judgmental mush, too many Americans have become incapable of facing the brutal reality of unprovoked hatred, based on envy, resentment and ultimately on a vicious urge to lash out against others for the pain of one's own insignificance. That has been a common thread in things as disparate as ghetto riots, two world wars, and now Islamic terrorism.

One example to apply the divergent nature of worldviews as they are applied to morality and values is to look at the concepts of tolerance and diversity from the two world perspectives. Both worldviews believe in these principles but each articulates the values from distinctly differing perspectives and moral bases. The Humanistic/Synthetic view tolerance as meaning those who disagree with their opinions or the way they see an issue must be tolerant of the viewpoint, are not allowed to argue their counter perception of what is right and most certainly must not pass judgment. If they do so it is seen as an attack and intolerant. But if those with the Humanistic/Synthetic vision are asked to be tolerant of an opposing point of view they see it as a moral affront to what they perceive as being right. This is because the Humanistic/Synthetic perceive their point of view as accurate and beyond challenge.

Diversity is seen by the Humanistic/Synthetic mind as a phrase that implies special consideration for certain groups that the Humanistic/Synthetic have deemed worthy. These special groups are given extra benefits and opportunities and are told to use other groups as a scapegoat for any and all problems they have faced.

On the other hand the Universal/Natural worldview defines and applies tolerance and diversity as a literal adaptation of the word. To the Universal/Natural, tolerance means openness for all ideas and points of view no matter how unpalatable they may be; while diversity means openness to many backgrounds and cultural influences within a framework of equality. They apply such a definition because of a fundamental reliance on a higher authority. In essence, any difference of opinion is not worrisome because it does not change the universal order of morality. Thus, the Universal/Natural honors Voltaire's famous quote stating, "I disapprove of what you say, but I will defend to the death your right to say it".

Hopefully after looking at the examples on tolerance and diversity one will see the way in which an individual perceives the world has a compelling impact in the way they apply and push forward their opinions and agendas.

It is clear that the development and perception of morality is a key in understanding how individuals acquire their worldview.

To summarize the issue of morality, James Q. Wilson offered a clear example of the difference between the Humanistic/Synthetic vision of morality that is promoted by self-proclaimed intellectuals as opposed to the moral underpinnings of the Universal/Natural found in the general public:

> There can scarcely be anything worth calling a moral sense if people can be talked out of it by modern philosophy, secular humanism, Marxist dialectics, or psudo-Freudian psychoanalysis. But I doubt that most people most of the time are affected by these intellectual fashions. The intellectuals who consume them may be affected. If they think life is without moral reasoning, they may live accordingly, creating an avant- garde in which "meaning" is to be found in self-expressive art, a bohemian counterculture, or anarchistic politics. But the lives of most people are centered around the enduring facts of human existence—coping with a family, establishing relationships, and raising children.

Morality

Humanistic/Synthetic   **Universal/Natural**

Pre-conventional/Conventional morality   Post-conventional morality
Egocentric judgment   Principled judgment
Relativist orientation   Social contracts
Quid pro quo   Universality
Expectations   Logical comprehensiveness/
                                            ethics

"Can I"   "Should I"
Scientific utopias   Equality of institutions
Eugenic   Universal moral truths
Nihilistic   Natural laws—society
Man is autonomous   Higher order—power
Lack of deference to a higher power   Religion/salvation
Moral relativity   Morality of greater society
Moral equivalency   Realize evil
Secular Humanist   Religious society
Individual morality   Tolerance
Do not accept evil   Diversity
Group-think
Blind diversity
Blind tolerance
Narcissism

4

NEEDS

"To understand the world one must not be worrying about one's self."—Albert Einstein

The second arena that effects the development of one's world vision also comes to us from the field of Psychology. The understanding of human needs and the behavior that corresponds to having our needs fulfilled is closely tied to determining what worldview will develop within each of us. The reason for this is that our behaviors are the result of motivations and basic drives that take place in order to meet our needs. Thus one determinant in shaping worldviews is found in the question of how needs are met. This plays a fundamental role not only in the way we view the world, but in how we adapt to it. In order to understand how the concept of needs operates in humans we must begin by looking at the theory of needs.

Psychologist Abraham Maslow developed a theory called the Hierarchy of Needs in which he ranked human needs, one above the other, into five levels. The most basic needs are found at the bottom of the hierarchy with progressively more specialized needs found as one moves up the continuum in a stair like fashion symbolizing personal growth.

Maslow's Hierarchy of Needs:

> *Level 5*—Self-actualization needs: self-fulfillment, self growth, uniqueness.

Level 4—Esteem needs: self-respect, recognition, self-esteem, status, prestige.

Level 3—Love needs: acceptance, love, friendship, understanding.

Level 2—Safety needs: structure, order, security, protection, freedom from fear.

Level 1—Physiological needs: food, water, air and warmth.

Individuals begin at level 1. As one level of needs is attained by self or outside sources one moves up to the next level and so on until the ultimate goal is reached, that being self actualization. The behavior that humans exhibit in order to have these needs met is the key to understanding the connection that Maslow's hierarchy has to the development of world views

The needs found in Maslow's hierarchy can be met by either an intrinsic locus/mode of control or an extrinsic locus/mode of control. The locus of control is defined by the way we act or have our needs met. If the needs are met with an intrinsic locus, a person is in fact meeting their own needs. When the locus is extrinsic a person is allowing someone else or something else to fill the needs. Worldview development takes place moving from Humanistic/Synthetic to Universal/Natural as one learns to meet their needs and become self-actualized.

Self-actualization is achieved by not giving others power to control your needs and thus your mental state. Self-actualization can only occur when one meets all of their needs. To achieve self actualization, power is not given to others, instead it is given to a higher power or universal order that allows for acceptance of self and the ability to mentally grow beyond the lower level needs to achieve a distinct cognitive understanding of the world. It carries with it an understanding of our humanity and place in the universe that is humbled. In other words, becoming self-actualized is in a sense becoming everything to you and yet nothing compared to the universe.

This is not to say that a self-actualized individual lives a life void of relationships, interaction and strong emotional attachments with others. The phrase, "man is not an island", is true; but it is the distinction of what constitutes that which is outside the island that man needs or must belong to that is primary to understanding self actualization. For the self actualized man, the external partner is a power that transcends other men; while to those who are not self actualized, the external partner is found in other people or material things. Man is indeed a social animal and more often than not decides to allow others to meet needs and represent important external control structures. Even the self-actualized individual has the capacity and some might say the genetic need to live within the framework of social interaction. But the key difference is that the self-actualized person understands the ultimate necessity to be self-accountable based upon a fundamental faith in a power greater than their fellow man.

For instance, the self-actualized Tibetan monk can withstand unthinkable cold for hours without harm to their bodies because primary physiological needs are connected to their faith in a higher order. Likewise, the martial arts master can undertake feats of superhuman strength and power without harm to life or limb because their focus is beyond the here and now which allows for a flow of consciousness that harnesses a power greater than self. These tasks are not easily undertaken but they are not all that uncommon.

Those who are progressing up Maslow's hierarchy and are meeting their own needs through an intrinsic locus would be members of the Universal/Natural vision. Those with the Humanistic/Synthetic vision have an extrinsic locus of control that allows other humans or material possessions to meet their needs and define them. The Humanistic/Synthetic live in a world where they look to the expectations of others to build a sense of self that is similar to Conventional morality discussed in chapter two.

The extrinsic based Humanistic/Synthetic worldview with its reliance on others allows for a greater amount of emotion to be brought into play. This happens because having an extrinsic locus of control gives others the power to meet needs or not. When others can take away needs they have been filling for you, pain and emptiness will result and emotions will run high. In fact the Humanistic/Synthetic vision is more highly emotionally charged in general than that of the Universal/Natural worldview which looks to faith and acceptance to allow for less emotional reactions to life's problems, issues or worldly questions.

For example, teenagers who allow their boy/girlfriend to meet the needs of love, acceptance and friendship are devastated as the result of a breakup in the relationship. Because needs were met extrinsically, the emotional toll is often severe as feelings of emptiness dominate. These feelings go away only as a result of having the lost needs met intrinsically or by allowing a new person or activity to fill them extrinsically.

This is not to say the Universal/Natural is unable to experience the rainbow of human emotions. Perceptual ability is however much more developed in the

Universal/Natural worldview where emotions can be more readily placed in a less severe context. The example of a monk exposed to the cold or a martial arts master breaking concrete details the ability for one to remove painful emotions from the equation.

Emotions are defined as a person's feelings based on their view of the situation. The Humanistic/Synthetic thinker who views situations based on a lack of power or control will respond in purely emotional ways; while the Universal/Natural thinker who has met their own needs and has placed faith, trust and reason upon the situation will show less emotion if any at all. Not that the Universal/Natural is emotionless, cold or mean spirited, it is just that they view the problems, issues and worldly questions from a set of assumptions that offers acceptance and balance more readily than that of the Humanistic/Synthetic mind set.

For the Universal/Natural mind passion without principal is just emotion. To the Humanistic/Synthetic, emotion is misread as principled thought. The Universal/Natural perceives the world based on rational principles while the Humanistic/Synthetic perceives the world based on emotional ideals. Emotions for the Universal/Natural are more often what one would deem positive in nature, while the emotions of the Humanistic/Synthetic would be seen as negative. For example, the loss of a loved one is filled with highly charged emotions for the Humanistic/Synthetic while the Universal/Natural is apt to be more stoic in their reaction as a result of an acceptance in the natural order of the life cycle.

Another example will help clear up any confusion. If one rides a roller coaster the ride will either be scary or fun, depending on the riders perception of the situation. If you give power to the ride and do not analyze what is going to be happening, the ride will control your emotions and be scary. On the other hand if you analyze the ride and look at the situation in a reasoned manner, the ride will not be given power to control your negative emotions and will be fun. To the Humanistic/Synthetic mind, life is an out of control roller coaster filled with screams and tears. To the Universal/Natural mind, life is a roller coaster that is fun, challenging and has its ups and downs.

It could be argued that everything is scary the first time, even to a stoic, but we must be reminded of the martial artist attempting to break the concrete block. Success is only possible if fear is removed, and the expectancy value for success is 100%. In other words, the task is and has been successful in the mind of the martial artist before the attempt. If the artist allows fear to enter the equation, the attempt will result in the inability to drive the hand through the block. This will be followed by the realization of pain that comes with bouncing one's hand off the surface of concrete.

Any discussion on needs must be coupled with an analysis of motivation in our human nature. James Ramsey Ullman summed up motivation as it applies to the Humanistic/Synthetic: "We are so clothed in rationalization and dissemblance that we can recognize but dimly the deep primal impulses that motivate us." The Universal/Natural worldview perceives motivation as based on what Jeremy Bentham called "The governance of two sovereign masters, pain and pleasure." In other words we do what gives us pleasure and avoid what gives us pain. Thus to avoid allowing our human nature to act in its primitive sense, the Universal/Natural vision is guided by the incentives, both pleasurable and painful, that social institutions place on man's decision making process. These constraints modify and control man by working with his nature as a pain/pleasure animal. The self actualized Universal/Natural mind avoids pain by eliminating desire for worldly acceptance or material possessions, while the Humanistic/Synthetic mind focuses on external worldly acceptance and material possessions, thus causing more emotional unrest than is necessary.

The Humanistic/Synthetic worldview may agree with Bentham but do not think the incentives of external institutions are necessary to control man. They believe man can control himself even though there is a denial of human nature and an external locus of control that gives others the power to meet needs and thus control emotions in a negative way.

David Reisman touched on the issue of intrinsic and extrinsic control when he suggested there are broadly two kinds of political people. "Gyroscopic people have internal guidance systems. Radar people steer according to signals bounced off others." This again exemplifies the differences in the perception of needs between the two worldviews. Needs are met internally in the "Gyroscopic" worldview of the Universal/Natural, while they are met externally in the "Radarscopic" world of the Humanistic/Synthetic.

The image of self esteem, self concept and self respect that each world view holds is another important piece of the puzzle in defining the conditions that take one person to the Humanistic/Synthetic vision while another goes toward the Universal/Natural view. Webster's dictionary may be helpful in explaining. When describing self-esteem, one of the definitions given is "self-conceit", while another definition is the word "pride", meaning a reasonable or justifiable self-respect. When looking at the concept of self-esteem the Humanistic/

Synthetic thinker lives in a world of self-conceit while the Universal/Natural thinker lives in a world of self-respect.

Self-esteem is defined by the Humanistic/Synthetic as how worthwhile we are, based on what others think. That is not the total picture however, because the Humanistic/Synthetic also have an external focus for defining self. This is based not on any specific achievement but on a non-judgmental vision of absolute acceptance regardless of behavior. In other words they need the acceptance of Conventional morality but within a framework of non-judg-mental moral anarchy. The result of this vision can be seen in the social struc-ture, created over the last 40 years, that tells every individual they are great no matter what they say or do. This occurs even if the behavior of the individual is beyond the bounds of acceptable social norms. The end result is a person who acts as if they have a high self-esteem even if there is no reason. In fact, the high self esteem of school children who are praised and rewarded for any and all behaviors, even if the actions are commonplace, silly or outright wrong, has created a prison population that is full of individuals with high self esteem and low moral character.

Self esteem for the Universal/Natural is defined as how worthwhile we are based on measurable achievements an individual has accomplished. These achievements build an internal sense of positive self-esteem as the result of actually doing something. The end result is a person whose self-esteem is gen-uine. Feeling good about one's self as the result of accomplishing a difficult task is far different than feeling full of yourself as the result of someone telling you how great you are.

Self-concept is based on aligning what others think of us with what we think about ourselves. The Humanistic/Synthetic's external focus causes the self-concept to be controlled by outside forces and thus it is often aligned with reality in a negative way. An example might be an individual diagnosed with anorexia nervosa or depression who see themselves in a distorted way and thus have a poor self-concept. The Universal/Natural's internal focus causes the self-concept to be more in line with what external perceptions are and thus is more often aligned in a positive way. An example might be a person who accepts the general consensus that they are physically attractive because they eat healthy, exercise and fit the guidelines for body weight and height set by respected health professionals.

Lastly, self-respect, which is the level of personal standards one places on self and thus demands others reciprocate, is greater in the Universal/Natural worldview. This is due to the fact that self-esteem based on achievement and self-concept based on perceptual reality allows for strength of character that formulates into a high degree of self-respect. For the Humanistic/Synthetic vision control is external so the ability to hold oneself to a high level of respect is counter to their perception of the world and thus causes a lack of self-respect. In other words, the Humanistic/Synthetic is willing to lower their personal standards of behavioral respect to secure even the most disrespectful human interaction in order to have their needs met. As a result, choices inconsistent with the concept of self-respect have become commonplace in behaviors related to sexual activities, violence and a host of what used to be considered deviant lifestyles.

As you can see the psychology associated with the meeting of needs plays a vital role in the development of worldviews. Behaviors that stem from a misalignment in the fulfillment of needs can and does cause the erosion of civilized interaction between members of society. Understanding needs and appropriately acting upon that knowledge will create a best-case scenario for the maintenance of civilization.

Needs

Humanistic/Synthetic	Universal/Natural
Extrinsic locus of control	Intrinsic locus of control
Emotional	Meet own needs
Man can control himself	Acceptance of self
Self conceit	Faith/acceptance over emotions
Emotion shows principle	Controlled by external incentives
Emotional ideals	Self-respect
"Radarscopic"	Emotion= passion with principles
Lack of self-respect	Rational principles
Misaligned reality= poor self esteem	"Gyroscopic"

5

LEARNING

"If you're treated a certain way you become a certain kind of person. If certain things are described to you as being real they're real for you whether they're real or not."—James Baldwin

Learning plays a large role in the divergent perceptions of the world. Chapter 5 will look at the concept of how man learns and connect it with the question as to why one person acquires one particular worldview and another aligns with the opposite view of the world. The focus of this chapter will be to look at the types and stages of learning and see how they impact the two worldviews. By understanding the learning process we will continue to explain where the schism occurs that separates our binary perceptions of how the world operates.

There are 4 ways in which man acquires knowledge and learns to expand his cognitive abilities: Classical conditioning, operant conditioning, social learning and cognitive learning.

Classical conditioning is best known by Ivan Pavlov's salivating dog experiments. It is learning by associating a environmental stimulus with an unrelated internal response or behavior. For example, there may have been a time when soon after you ate a particular food you came down with a virus that made you violently sick. From that day forward you acquired a food aversion to the specific food you ate. Now you can't even see the food or smell it without feeling nauseous. The food aversion is real even though what you ate does not actually make someone sick.

The second type of learning comes through operant learning and the theories of B.F Skinner. Operant learning is learning that comes by our actions and the consequences of those actions. It is learning based on reinforcements both positive and negative that shape our behavior through reward and punishment. An example of operant conditioning is seen in the workplace. If you work hard and are rewarded, intrinsically with a promotion or increased responsibilities or extrinsically by getting a raise, the reinforcement will motivate you to continue to work hard. In other words the behavior you exhibited was responded to and that caused the behavior to be repeated. In economic theory this would be likened to creating incentives through supply and demand to modify behavior in the marketplace. Another example can be seen when looking at dating. If you asked a girl out and were denied, you would be far less likely to ask out another. In short, Operant learning takes place through operation with your environment.

The next way in which we learn is socially. Social learning theory comes to us from Albert Bandura. It is learning that is acquired through observation. An example of social learning is a child watching a parent arguing and yelling at another adult; later the child yells and argues with a sibling as a method of communication. Social learning covers a vast array of cognitive processes that assimilate each of us into the mainstream of the social fabric.

Lastly, cognitive learning rounds out the list of the four ways in which we learn. Cognitive learning is a continuation of social learning but is vastly different in methodology. While social learning is fairly passive and deals with taking in learning through the senses, cognitive learning is an active self-controlling activity. Cognitive learning deals with mental processes and is the most difficult type of learning process. To grow using cognitive learning one must think abstractly and with reason, analysis, synthesis and evaluation. For example, NASA has to utilize cognitive learning to determine why the Space Shuttle Columbia disintegrated upon reentry. The ability to think critically leads to higher order living, learning and the articulation of principles like Post conventional morality or self-actualization. In short, cognitive learning is thinking with reason.

An example of cognitive learning would be making a decision between several choices through reason by using data, projection, cause and effect, cost analysis and a myriad of other quantifiable methods to make a critical choice while understanding the costs involved and having a best case scenario of the results. This would be done internally and without interference by emotions, selfish motives or denial.

Now that we have discussed the ways in which we acquire knowledge we need to connect that understanding to how it affects our worldviews. Conditioning, operant learning and social learning all have an external locus of control and are passive in their approach. These learning methods are counter to cognitive learning that has an internal locus of control and is highly demanding on the individual to take charge and critically analyze. In order to fully incorporate cognitive learning at the higher order levels one must not only have a fully developed mind they must in fact, use it. Thus, cognitive learning comes with time beyond the more readily acquired leanings that stem from classical conditioning, operant conditioning and social learning.

It is consistent with the theories put forth thus far to connect the worldview of the Humanistic/Synthetic mind with a mind most utilized and developed through conditioning, both classical and operant as well as through social learning. On the opposite end of the spectrum, one finds the Universal/Natural vision. The Universal/Natural utilizes cognitive learning to a greater extent in terms of far reaching principles where previous knowledge developed by the external modes of learning has been enriched through strenuous cognitive efforts.

To further the discussion on the development of worldviews the theories of cognitive development offered by Jean Piaget need to be added to the equation. According to Piaget, humans move through four stages of cognitive development.

1. Sensorimotor: (Age birth-2) Stage based on sensation and movement where pleasure and pain associations are made. Mental images are associated with symbols. Stage of self centered world based on ones individual reference point.

2. Pre-operational: (Age2-7) Stage based on illogical and unreasoned operations with the world. View world in terms of him/herself. Unable to see other points of view.

3. Concrete operations: (Age 7-11) Stage based on a world that is concrete/real. Has the ability to reason at low level. Difficult to see other points of view.

4. Formal operations: (Age 11-on) Stage based on highly symbolic thoughts, logic, philosophy, mathematics, ethics and scientific facts. Deal with subjects like truth, justice and fairness.

Piaget's stages of cognitive development fit well into understanding the development process of acquiring one's world view as they clearly show a progression of mental capacities. It could be argued that the stages mimic Kohlberg's moral development stages with the Sensorimotor and Pre-operational stages closely matching Pre-conventional moral development, Concrete operations aligning with Conventional morality and Formal operations connected to Post-conventional morality. With that said, the perceptions of the Humanistic/Synthetic would best fit within the Concrete operational stage of Piaget's model while the Universal/Natural vision would be aligned with the development of Formal operations.

Piaget's cognitive development theory also aligns itself with the ways in which we learn as previously outlined with Sensorimotor tied to classical conditioning, Pre-operational tied to operant learning, Concrete operations tied to social learning and Formal operations tied to cognitive learning. Clearly there is a connection between the developmental processes humans must progress through and the development of one's worldview. The Humanistic/Synthetic perception of the world is most closely aligned with Social learning, Conventional morality and Concrete operations while the Universal/Natural model most closely resembles Cognitive learning, Post-conventional morality and Formal operations.

Piaget's age distinctions are important to point out but humans do not move through developmental levels at exactly the same time and there are wide differences in maturation. In fact, the process of growing up developmentally is not an easy task that happens without personal effort. What is important to point out is that the Universal/Natural worldview is a more highly developed perceptual model of the world which is based on a far greater mastery of the processes that Kohlberg and Piaget have so masterfully laid out.

It must be said that there is a transition that people must pass as they move from external learning to internal but in terms of the developmental processes that take place and impact one's worldview it is clear that learning plays a vital role.

What then happens to someone who holds a Humanistic/Synthetic worldview when they are confronted with a cognitive argument? What happens when empirical data, reason, projection, cause and effect, cost analysis and a myriad of other quantifiable methods to explain a critical choice is given? Do they take into consideration the costs and give a best case scenario of the results?

This very question was discussed earlier in the text and it is now an appropriate time to consider the issue. The response to the aforementioned question is that a person will go through what is known as cognitive dissonance. A person with a Humanistic/Synthetic worldview will fight to avoid dealing with the conflicting information because to question their worldview is a very uncomfortable proposition. It is uncomfortable because it forces the person to open their mind in ways that are counter to the usual methods of learning and thinking. As a result, the person will deflect the information in order to remain in a cognitive realm that they are more comfortable with. To better understand this mental riddle we must look closely at cognitive dissonance theory.

Dissonance Theory was developed by Leon Festinger in 1957. At the heart of the theory lies the rationale as to why productive dialogue for personal change is difficult for the Humanistic/Synthetic vision. In brief, cognitive dissonance occurs when one is presented with an attitude, emotion, behavior, value or opinion that is at odds with one's current set of beliefs, knowledge structure or worldview. As a result, cognitive dissonance causes a person to have psychological tension similar to hunger or thirst; and as an outcome of this reactive state, the person will exhibit basic drive like behavior to eliminate the discomfort.

In order to reduce the dissonance or tension, a person will choose to do one of three things. One option is that they will add a consonant or similar cognition, thus attaching more weight to the earlier discrepant and ease the tension. The second option is that they may change the cognition in order to make it consistent with their intellectual reality or modify the internal or external cognition to moderate and compromise the mental discrepancy. The last option is that they may alter the importance of the first discrepancy and ease the tension by rationalizing that the first idea offered was insignificant and incapable of having merit.

Unfortunately, the basic instincts of human nature usually win out in regard to these choices. People tend to ease the tension of cognitive dissonance by discrediting the information as unimportant in relation to the beliefs they hold. Instead of looking to add additional weight and credibility to the information that caused the cognitive dissonance or compromise intellectually, individuals go on the attack much like an animal who has not eaten for days. When one places this theory in relation to producing positive dialogue for personal change the results are often deficient.

Cognitive dissonance is seen in worldview development because instead of acquiring new beliefs and changing the mental balance of cognition towards personal understanding and developmental growth, the Humanistic/Synthetic mind will act to reduce or remove the importance of the idea that caused the dissonance. It is much easier to discredit an idea than it is to adjust one's mind-set or worldview. The result of this behavioral reality can be seen in the negative reaction that takes place after new or divergent ideas are presented to the Humanistic/Synthetic. Since cognitive learning is a difficult mental undertaking, it is easier to rationalize the information presented as incorrect.

Instead of civility and rationale discussion, the Humanistic/Synthetic will assault, retaliate and repudiate any and all possible opinions that are at odds with their current set of beliefs. The emotional reaction to differing models of thought to alleviate cognitive dissonance has become particularly nasty and mean spirited in regard to the diverse viewpoints presented as an attempt to better our society. Incivility and the inability to discuss viable ideas and compromise for the betterment of shared social institutions is a result of the cognitive dissonance inherent in the Humanistic/Synthetic vision that uses insults and viscously slanderous rhetoric in lieu of reasoned thought.

Of course some are in transition between the Humanistic/Synthetic and Universal/Natural worldviews. Clearly we sometimes see mean spirited dialogue coming from the Universal/Natural. This happens as a result of the person being in the early transitional phase toward a Universal/Natural mind where the vestiges of their old Humanistic/Synthetic worldview have surfaced.

A quote by Isaac Asimov furthers this discussion:

> Suppose that we are wise enough to learn and know—and yet not wise enough to control our learning and knowledge, so that we use it to destroy ourselves? Even if that is so, knowledge remains better than ignorance. It is better to know—even if the knowledge endures only for the moment that comes before destruction—than to gain eternal life at the price of a dull and swinish lack of comprehension of a universe that swirls unseen before us in all its wonder. That was the choice of Achilles, and it is mine, too.

As you can see, cognitive dissonance can be a wall that hinders personal growth, discussion and theory outlined in this text.

There is another factor that must be taken into account within the discussion of why the development of worldviews is difficult to understand. This stems from the fact that individuals, more often than not, are unaware of the complexity of formulating complex thought processes gained by cognitive learning. In other words, they are not very smart. Francis Bacon exemplified this concept: "There is a difference between happiness and wisdom: he that thinks himself the happiest man is really so; but he that thinks himself the wisest is generally the greatest fool." Winston Groom and Davis Roth also touched on this theory when creating the movie Forrest Gump. In the movie an unnamed character asks Forrest Gump, "Are you stupid or something?" wherein Forrest Gump replies, "My mama always said, stupid is as stupid does."

The developmental process of acquiring information, processing that information and then applying knowledge is used to differing degrees and to varying capacities within each worldview. The determining factor is the amount of cognitive learning that is taking place. A result of these differences is what will be termed Gump's Law. It is a theory that applies to the Humanistic/Synthetic worldview.

Before further details of the theory are laid out it is important to explain that the premise of Gump's Law is not meant to be critical or mean spirited. The theory only explains how the developmental stage of the Humanistic/Synthetic worldview manifests itself in terms of self-awareness. Remember the development of a worldview is a process of time and place associated with numerous internal and external factors. Thus, it is not possible to avoid at some time having Gump's Law apply to each of us. This may be difficult to hear and cognitive dissonance may be the result but hopefully the reader will contemplate the analysis with the highest of academic thought.

Sometimes the most insightful theories are also the most simplistic. Gump's Law is no different, it states:

1. *Those who think they are the most intelligent are actually the most ignorant*

2. *Those who are the most ignorant are the last ones to know it.*

3. *The last to know will act as if what they know is intelligent.*

In more unadorned terms Gump's law states that the dumb think they are smart because they are so dumb they don't know how dumb they are.

As you can see Gump's Law works in a cyclical manner like a computer stuck in a program loop. Once Gump's Law is applied to an individual it is hard to break from the pattern. Only through the cognitive learning process can one move beyond the blind perceptions of Gump's Law. Many who hold the Humanistic/Synthetic worldview are sure their beliefs are accurate and will emotionally fight for the vision they hold. Unfortunately those with this perception of the world around them are blind to the possibility that another way of looking at the world exists. It is commonplace to hear someone passionately argue a point of view that is so obviously based on incorrect facts or illogical assumptions; yet they do so without even the slightest inkling that what they are saying is ignorant, not to mention embarrassing.

The phrase, "teenagers don't know what they don't know yet", is a telling example of Gump's Law and the movement towards a Universal/Natural worldview. Anyone who has ever come to the realization of how ignorant their thinking was during their teen years has begun the process of moving to the Universal/Natural worldview. Sadly for many, this realization of ignorance never develops. As a result, the Humanistic/Synthetic adult is perpetually stuck in a frame of reference void of the wondrous journey the lack of cognitive awareness motivates one to embark upon.

Gump's Law is not a new concept since several great thinkers touched on the law with varying degrees of philosophical bent. Benjamin Disraeli said: "To be conscious that you are ignorant is a great step to knowledge." Plato said: "Herein is the evil of ignorance, that he who is neither good nor wise is nevertheless satisfied with himself: he has no desire for that of which he feels no want." Rousseau reminded us: "The risk is not in what he does not know, but in what he thinks he knows." Locke stated: "Knowledge being to be had of visible and certain truth, error is not a fault of our knowledge, but a mistake of our judgment, giving assent to that which is not true." Lastly, Leo Tolstoy stated; "When ignorance does not know something, it says that what it does not know is stupid."

Thomas Sowell has pointed out that each vision regards the other as mistaken. The Humanistic/Synthetic worldview perceives those with the Universal/Natural worldview as having less morality and intelligence than they have acquired. They believe those with a Universal/Natural vision are a moral outrage and are in deliberate opposition to the common good. Thus the views expressed by the Universal/Natural are seen as having little use because the thoughts of the Humanistic/Synthetic are of course blindly accurate.

In contrast, Sowell states that those with a Universal/Natural worldview see those with a Humanistic/Synthetic vision as well meaning but mistaken and unrealistic in their assumptions. They see the Humanistic/Synthetic vision holders as moral and intelligent people who simply do not understand their limits in a dynamic universe. In other words, the Humanistic/Synthetic's perceptual universe is hindered by Gump's Law until the time comes when reasoning ability is increased through cognitive effort.

The mistaken notion of what constitutes knowledge or intellectual strength must be understood in terms beyond the traditional if one is to grasp the Universal/Natural worldview. Once again, Thomas Sowell articulates the discussion regarding knowledge and learning:

> Considering the enormous range of human knowledge, from intimate personal knowledge of specific individuals to the complexities of organizations and the subtleties of feelings, it is remarkable that one speck in this firmament should be the sole determinant of whether someone is considered knowledgeable or ignorant in general. Yet it is a fact of life that an unlettered person is considered ignorant, however much he may know about nature and man, and a Ph.D. is never considered ignorant, however barren his mind might be outside his narrow specialty and however little he grasps about human feeling or social complexities.

John Locke also had an opinion on the lettered and well read. "Reading furnishes the mind only with materials for knowledge; it is thinking that makes what we read ours." "Till a man can judge whether they be truths or not, his understanding is but little improved, and thus men of much reading, though greatly learned, but may be little knowing."

It is obvious that the two worldviews are not only opposed in a theoretical sense but they are at odds with each other in coming to terms with accepting that both visions exist. Developing an understanding of one's worldview in conjunction with the fact that another view exists creates a problematic situation. This can only be solved if one is willing to open up a channel of neurological capabilities before unused and delve into the many nuances of the developmental process that this text discusses. Without a willingness to begin a process of personal growth the two worldviews will continue to be at odds with each other and positive change will fester behind name-calling and ignorant chest beating.

At some point in time anyone who wants to move away from the Humanistic/Synthetic worldview must begin the process of cognitive growth. This can only happen as a result of taking it upon oneself to search for the truth by reading diverse opinions and scientific research as well as listening to what social and political leaders are offering. Far too many only hear and repeat the social catch phrase of the day. Because it is easier to just follow leaders who spin a yarn of acceptable social thought than to truly listen and evaluate the thoughts spewed out in the marketplace of ideas that some call the mass media. Only after a careful sifting through the facts and rhetoric can one begin to come to some conclusions that align with the real world and not a utopian one.

In summary, the ways in which we learn, process and apply what our minds can perceive and articulate plays a vital role in the development of our world visions. To ignore the fundamental ramifications of an analysis into understanding why we think the way we do and then apply that thinking to our perception of the world has been one of the fatal flaws in man's ability to maintain the progress of civilized social organization.

Learning

Humanistic/Synthetic

Conditioning-classical and operant
Social learning
Concrete operations
External/passive locus of control
Cognitive dissonance
Gump's Law
Moral outrage

Universal/Natural

Cognitive learning
Internal locus of control
Formal operations
Empirical reasoning
Quantifiable data, projection, cause
and effect, cost analysis

6

POWER

"The fundamental concept in social science is Power, in the same sense in which Energy is the fundamental concept in physics."—Bertrand Russell

Russell was absolutely correct in his assumptions concerning the role power has on any comprehensive look at society. Thus, to continue our analysis on worldview development we must include the subject of power and detail its impact on our perceptions of how the world best functions.

Power is a common word we use and act upon in our social fabric, yet is is also one of the most misunderstood and misused concepts found within cultures. In order to fully understand power and its effects on worldview development we must first set up some definitions and explain some basic concepts.

Power is a universal experience. In a pure sense, power is submission by voluntary or involuntary compliance with another person. There are seven types of power and four laws of power that can be seen and utilized within the framework of the social sciences:

Types of Power:

1. *Legitimate*: Power is gained because a position held or the hierarchy found in an organization.

   Example: President, CEO.

2. *Information*: Power is gained because a person has knowledge you need or want to know or they have information you don't want them to have.

   Example: secretary, ex-girlfriend.

3. *Love*: Power is gained because a person can give it and/or you need it.

   Example: mother, spouse.

4. *Reward*: Power is gained because a person can give you something.
Example: boss, teacher.

5. *Punish*: Power is gained because a person can hurt or take something away from you.
Example: totalitarian dictator, parent.

6. *Expertise*: Power is gained because a person has a skill and can do something you can't and want to have done.
Example: plumber, computer technician.

7. *Referent*: Power is gained through force of personality, cognizance of argument, values and respect for the individual.
Example: Abraham Lincoln, Mohandas Gandhi, Martin Luther King, Jr.

When looking at the seven types of power, the power to punish is the most negative style for acquiring power. Even though there are certain times that use of it is necessary. Five of the types; Legitimate, Information, Love, Reward and Expertise have the potential to be either a negative or positive style for acquiring power. Only one type, Referent power, is seen as almost always being a positive way to acquire power. This is important to note because we will see that how power is perceived and which types of behaviors are used to acquire power is paramount in uncovering the developmental process of building one's worldview. A footnote on Referent power needs to be added here. If Referent behaviors are used to acquire power without the components of universal values and respect for the individual, it can be misused. An example is the behavior of Adolph Hitler who used Referent behaviors to acquire power and then used punishment to maintain control of the people.

The next but no less important piece of information concerns how power operates within the social arena deals with the four laws of power. Of all the mistaken notions that humans seem to have, not understanding and applying the laws of power properly are the most erroneous.

Laws of power:

1. *All power is given.*
Example: Teachers think they have power but students ultimately decide if they will follow the teacher.

2. *The more power you give, the more you are given.*
Example: Teachers who give intrinsic rewards or admit mistakes are given power by students.

3. *Power is not held*; it is what you say and do that makes others give you power.

Example: Teachers who know what they are talking about and create a productive classroom are given power by students.

4. *Once you believe you hold power, you begin the process of having power taken away from you.*

Example: Once a teacher "looses it", pulls rank and gives unwarranted punishment to a student, the other students lose respect and remove power previously given to the teacher.

John Kenneth Galbraith understood the first law of power: "Perhaps the oldest and certainly the wisest strategy for the exercise of power is to deny that it is possessed."

Note that these four laws are not difficult to comprehend but seem to be the most troublesome to carry out for individuals. This takes us to the heart of the matter as we look at power and worldviews. Those with the Humanistic/Synthetic vision recognize power as the opposite of these four laws. They see power as held and feel the need to hold any power they feel they possess very tightly. The Humanistic/Synthetic world vision does not see power as connected to what one says or does, so words and actions can be utilized to any accord they see fit. An example would be for the Humanistic/Synthetic to lie in order to get a desired end because the end will justify the means. Lastly the Humanistic/Synthetic excuse rule number four because they will use any means necessary to hold onto the power that is given to them even if that means exhibiting behaviors that are purely negative in nature. In fact, the more power that is perceived as being taken away from the Humanistic/Synthetic, the more they will fight to hold it and the more dangerous they become.

The Humanistic/Synthetic vision will also try to maintain control and power over others at any cost by misusing the seven types of powers mentioned previously. This is a dangerous application of power and its ramifications are well known. Examples include Hitler, Stalin, Pol Pot, Mao, Castro as well parents, teachers, preachers and contemporary politicians who have a Humanistic/Synthetic worldview and thus misuse and abuse the constructs of power against their fellow man.

Jacques Maritain understood the abuse of power, and thus added a crucial component to defining power appropriately:

> Power is the force by means of which you can oblige others to obey you. Authority is the right to direct and command, to be listened to or obeyed by others. Authority requests power. Power without authority is tyranny.

Lord Acton had an equally powerful definition: "Power tends to corrupt, and absolute power corrupts absolutely." Montesquieu also added depth to our understanding of power and its inherent risks: "Every man invested with power is apt to abuse it…To prevent this abuse, it is necessary from the very nature of things that power should be a check to power."

When looking to answer the question of how power operates, the Humanistic/Synthetic mind believes it has control and holds power while the Universal/Natural mind believes that ultimate authority and power comes from a universal order above man and beyond his grasp. In short, The Universal/Natural perception of an external power greater than self is in stark opposition to the Humanistic/Synthetic perception that power is held internally by individuals.

Even many belonging to the Universal/Natural School of world perceptions do not fully understand and apply the rules and types of power correctly. This is probably due to the fact that power is so seductive. Just look at the behaviors of individuals who have been given as Andy Warhol said their "15 minutes of fame". Once someone gets a taste of fame and power their attitudes and behavior change to a mind set that attempts to hold onto any shred of power that was given to them. Understanding power comes down to a matter of degree and level of development in the other areas that have been outlined in this text.

The bottom line however is that the Humanistic/Synthetic vision has to a much greater extent an inaccurate understanding of power and thus misuses it far more than the Universal/Natural thinker. This is because the very essence of the Humanistic/Synthetic perception is one that guides an individual from a blindly egocentric position based on a universal external acceptance that makes them feel they have control and thus hold power. Realizing the dangers of this perceptual worldview on the maintenance of civilization has perhaps been the biggest cultural calamity of the 20th century.

In the discussion of the two worldviews it is important to note once again that we are building a theoretical model based on the assumption that man is either in one school of thought or the other. For purposes of this text and for descriptive clarity, consistency to the worldview is assumed. However, it needs to be noted that there are sometimes gray areas that are produced when one is moving between one worldview towards another. To further clarify this ambiguous area it is important to note an important lesson from Thomas Sowell who after analyzing the two worldviews said that no one is 100% one vision or the other. The point is that the development of one's world view is a individual process and transformations occur over time which accounts for the intellectual inconsistencies that are sometimes seen.

With all of that said, one of the most problematic challenges facing the maintenance of civilization is to not allow the gray area to dominate social debate. If this is allowed to happen, vital social issues will be determined by intellectual inconsistency. Clearly, reasoned truths are hard to find when those who wield power are talking out of both sides of their mouths.

Although there may be some confusion and a lack of clarity on the subject of power, Thomas Sowell did express some of the fundamental differences in how each vision applies the concept. To the Humanistic/Synthetic the role of power is big. They see power as a tool the government should use to create social change. They view power as held by those who need to control the social structure. They do not see power as corrupting. On the other side of the spectrum, the Universal/Natural vision views the role of power as small. They see the exertion of power in social circumstances as a natural occurrence that is held in check by numerous factions and diverse special interests. It is a vision of power that is given yet can corrupt by its misuse.

What role does power play in the day to day operations of our civilization? The founding fathers warned us against the misuse of power. They built a nation conceived with the fundamental belief in the creation of a written Constitution. This document spelled out a separation of powers and a series of checks on the misuse of power within the governmental institution. Why did the founders create such a system? One reason is because James Madison understood man's human nature and his self-serving interest. Madison's brilliance was seen by his insight of power in working on the make-up of our constitutional system. In order to check abusive power, he came up with a system of governance that used factions, and the power they were given, to counter other factions thus canceling out the chances for abuse. In fact, power in the hands of those who would misuse it can happen throughout all of the social institutions. It is for this reason the role of power in perception and practice is important to understand in the context of worldviews.

Thomas Jefferson warned us about the abuse of power and detailed how leaders go about subverting liberty

> I have always found that rogues would be uppermost...These rogues set out with stealing the people's good opinion, and then steal from them the right of withdrawing it, by contriving laws and associations against the power of the people themselves.

Several other historical figures warned us about power and its effects upon man and society. They discuss and relate the components of power that defines one's worldview and show the difference in how each vision applies concepts in highly divergent ways. Francis Bacon told us: "It is a strange desire, to seek power, and to lose liberty; or to seek power over others, and to lose power over a man's self." James Baldwin connected power with morality: "The relationship of morality and power is a very subtle one. Because ultimately power without morality is no longer power." Cotvos looked at power and self: "All the power that we exercise over others depends on the power we exercise over ourselves." Lastly, Milton Friedman concluded two profound thoughts concerning power:

"Concentrated power is not rendered harmless by the good intentions of those who create it. The power to do good is also the power to do harm."

Power

Humanistic/Synthetic	Universal/Natural
Power is held	Power is given
Hold on to power	Give up power
Any action to acquire power	Words and deeds acquire power
Blind to power being removed	Remove power from corrupt
Maintain power at any cost	Authority requests power
Power means authority	Power will be abused
Power will not be abused	Power is external in universal order
Power is held internally	Role of power is small
Role of power is big	Separation of power
Power is tool to create social change	Checks and balances
Concentration of power	Power over self
Power over others	
Power controlled by man	

7

LEADERSHIP

"The chief executive who knows his strengths and weaknesses as a leader is likely to be far more effective than the one who remains blind to them. He also is on the road to humility—that priceless attitude of openness to life that can help a manager absorb mistakes, failures, or personal shortcomings."—John Adair

The next component in developing worldviews deals with the topic of leadership. As you might expect, the definition and application of leadership looks very different to each worldview.

For Niccolo Machiavelli the role of a leader was one in which the ends justified the means. In other words, what one does is of less importance than what is achieved. This does not mean that what is achieved is justifiable or right, only that the agenda put forth in the mind of the leader is correct. The Humanistic/Synthetic worldview is one that holds these same values. For example, the destructive behaviors and rhetoric shown by leaders who fought for universal health care in the 90's was irrelevant to them because it was far more important to accomplish their policy agenda than take into consideration the means used in the attempt to achieve socialized medicine.

Contrast this to what John Adair explains to us in the opening quote. He guides us to a philosophy that defines a leader as one who believes that the means justify the ends. In other words, what one does is of equal or greater importance than what is achieved. The Universal/Natural world vision is one that would subscribe to these ideals. For example, the means of civil disobedience shown by leaders who fought for civil rights in the 60's was just as important as achieving their policy agenda. In fact, the Universal/Natural see it as hypocritical to use means that are not aligned with the same principles that guide the ends.

Obviously the two views are at opposing ends of the spectrum and offer up an interesting look into how each worldview perceives the role of a leader in shaping society. So what is the true definition of leadership and how does the developmental process shape each of the two worldviews to apply such differing beliefs? The definition of leadership is to guide, conduct people, persuade, and serve as a way for others to follow. It is the capacity to instill values in others. In fact, values determine leadership and leadership is the major factor in cooperation. Values and principles play a vital role in proper leadership and thus one who does not or has not developed the values necessary to put forth leadership in a proper and just fashion may in fact accomplish something but it is done through avenues other than by true leadership.

Chester Barnard discussed leadership in eloquent terms by saying: "Leadership depends on followership." He went on to say that leadership: "Is viewed as a technological proficiency, combined with a moral complexity and a high degree of personal responsibility." He included in his assessment that a pivotal aspect of leadership is: "To inspire cooperative personal decisions by creating faith." Clearly, Barnard was discussing many of the personal attributes necessary in the developmental process that moves one to a Universal/Natural worldview.

According to Bernard, in order to develop leadership of the highest cognitive level one must show and project forth two vital aspects of leadership. One must have technical expertise in the form of training and education as well as the non-technical and theoretical moral base. This needs to be coupled with personal responsibility, not only to self, but also to the society as a whole. By personal responsibility we are talking about holding oneself to the highest standards of conduct and principles brought forth by a value system that comes from a humbled regard to natural laws above and beyond man. In other words, leadership is having the character to do the right thing even when nobody is watching.

The Humanistic/Synthetic mind may in fact have the technical expertise and believe they are subscribing to the aforementioned principles. However, their focus on the individual does not allow for the frame of reference needed to lead in a proper and defined way because the component of personal responsibility is lacking. Additionally, the Humanistic/Synthetic are short-term thinkers and reactive in nature to the problem solving process where action is based only in terms of the leaders ability to acquire additional power by acting on a problem after it has occurred. In essence, they act as if they have the answers and will fix the problem only after they are given the power to act. An example would be for a politician to come out after a problem arises and tell the people they will fix the problem by sponsoring a new piece of legislation with the caveat of having the people remember who "fixed" the problem the next election.

The Universal/Natural mind is more closely aligned with the principles of leadership as defined previously. Their perception of leadership may allow for behavior that is in accordance with universal moral underpinnings. In addition, they are long term thinkers and proactive in nature to the problem solving process where action is based in terms of the leader's ability to apply principles to foreseeable problems and then project solutions to circumvent their eventuality. An example would be for a politician to cut taxes because the economic stimulus will create jobs and raise government revenue thus increasing the standard of living for everyone.

To exemplify the difference in leadership roles one only has to look at how each type of leader acquires power. For the Universal/Natural worldview the use of referent power is paramount. The Humanistic/Synthetic worldview would more likely utilize punishment or reward power to get what they want. Ronald Reagan was given power because of his use of referent power against communism. Bill Clinton was given power by the National Education Association based on the monetary rewards the government could provide.

Why is leadership such a powerful component in understanding man's interaction with his environment? Leadership is the tool that applies one's worldview to the environment of social change. In fact, we give a great deal of power to our leaders because man has an inherent need to be lead. Ralph Waldo Emerson said: "Our chief want in life is somebody who will make us do what we can." Because of this, leadership as a concept has enormous ramifications to society. Obviously, the type of leader that is in charge will advance their worldview using differing styles of acquiring power. If this is done without a detailed understanding of why someone perceives the world the way in which they do, many a decision will be made that may not be in the best interests of society. In addition, leadership that arises from the acknowledgement of a power greater than self creates the balance so vitally needed to equalize the power and corruption inherent in man's nature.

In connecting the concept of leadership to the individual developmental process, several thoughts by Warren Bennis will draw some important conclusions. Hopefully these insights will give rise to the specific relationship between the human developmental process and the acquisition of one's world-view. Bennis said: "Becoming a leader is synonymous with becoming yourself. It is precisely that simple, and it is also that difficult." Clearly Bennis is talking about a style of leadership that is connected with the Universal/Natural vision in which the quest for self-actualization is a key component.

Bennis continues by offering a comparison between a manager and a leader:

> The manager administers; the leader innovates. The manager has a short-range view; the leader has a long-range perspective. The manager asks how and when; the leader asks what and why. The manager has his eye on the bottom line; the leader has his eye on the horizon. The manager accepts the status quo; the leader challenges it.

When comparing managers to leaders, Bennis is showing the difference between the Humanistic/Synthetic manager and the Universal/Natural leader.

Even Lord Byron seemed to effortlessly connect the development process with ones worldview: "When we think we lead we are most led." This quote relates to an earlier discussion on intelligence and how the Humanistic/Synthetic mind believes they can understand all things and in fact figure out what they cannot hope to know.

C.S. Lewis summed up the dangers of mistaken leadership and its effects on civilization when he made an observation applicable to those with the Humanistic/Synthetic worldview:

> Of all tyrannies, a tyranny exercised for the good of its victims may be the most oppressive. It may be better to live under robber barons than under omnipotent moral busybodies. The robber baron's cruelty may sometimes sleep, his cupidity may at some point be satiated; but those who torment us for our own good will torment us without end, for they do so with the approval of their own conscience.

On the opposite end of the spectrum, John Haggai summed up the Universal/Natural perception of leadership when he said:

> The leader seeks to communicate his vision to his followers. He captures their attention with his optimistic intuition of possible solutions to their needs. He influences them by the dynamism of his faith. He demonstrates confidence that the challenge can be met, the need resolved, the crisis overcome.

Leadership

Humanistic/Synthetic	Universal/Natural
Ends justify the means	Means justify the ends
Manager	Innovator/leader
Short range view	Long range view
Asks how and when	Asks what and why
Eye on bottom line	Eye on horizon
Status Quo	Challenges status quo
Omnipotent/omniscient	Humility
Reactive	Pro-active
	Values/principles/moral complexity
	Technical proficiency
	Influences by dynamism of faith
	Confidence
	Personal responsibility
	Optimistic intuition

8

THEOLOGY

"Morality without religion is only a kind of dead reckoning—an endeavor to find our place on a cloudy sea by measuring the distance we have run, but without any observation of the heavenly bodies."—Henry Wadsworth Longfellow

This chapter will deal with the sticky question of theology and its place in developing our worldview. The position of this text is not to say one worldview has a theological base and the other does not. The fundamental point to be detailed is that one worldview has an interpretation of theology vastly different than the other. This is important because perceptual differences between the two worldviews regarding theology will explain as well as answer many questions.

In uncovering one's worldview it is crucial to look at the relationship of self to the universe and the question of God's role in the dynamic nature of that universe. Each vision applies the role of God in very different ways with the Universal/Natural worldview accepting God's place in controlling the universe to a much greater extent than someone who holds the Humanistic/Synthetic worldview. An easy comparison would be to say that the Humanistic/Synthetic worldview holds a scientific vision of theology tempered by religion while the Universal/Natural worldview holds a religious vision of theology tempered by science.

To expand on this, the Humanistic/Synthetic worldview embraces a concept known as determinism based on random human genetic material or DNA while the Universal/Natural would comprehend it by a religious explanation such as predestination. It is not that the Universal/Natural does not accept DNA, only that they see DNA as a derivative of a larger universal force.

In the Universal/Natural vision the role of God and the acceptance that God is "above all things" is paramount. The Universal/Natural perception places man in an inferior role to God within a theological understanding to how and why the world works as it does. It is a vision that humbles itself to a higher order and does not believe it has the power to interfere with the natural order of God's plan or try to control nature. In other words the Universal/Natural vision understands that it plays a limited role against the unreachable power held by God. Man thus perceives his role as small and is held in check by forces far greater than he has the ability to master.

On the other hand the Humanistic/Synthetic worldview of theology perceives the role of God and the acceptance that God is above all as useful but limited. The Humanistic/Synthetic perception does not place man in an inferior role to God and does not look towards a theological understanding to how and why the world works as it does. It is a vision that does not humble itself to a higher order of things and does believe it has the power to interfere with the natural order of God's plan and control or at least modify a universal order. In other words the Humanistic/Synthetic vision does not understand and act as if it plays a limited role against an unreachable power held by God. Man under the Humanistic/Synthetic vision thus perceives his role as large and is not held in check by forces far greater than he has the ability to master.

Victor Davis Hanson adds to our understanding of the Humanistic/Synthetic vision of theology by defining what he calls the "arrogance of the Enlightenment", applying it to the current war on terror:

> This is the idea that all man's sins, all nature's problems and all the complexities of the cosmos can be alleviated by the god Reason, which they, almost alone, have embraced. They assume that if Americans werejust properly educated and trained, then we could insist on 100% excellence in this war—as if all wars are between absolute good and absolute evil, rather than a perennial struggle between the far better against the far worse, in which brutality like Dresden, Hiroshima, or Tet is to be avoided but nevertheless is not uncommon.

While both worldviews may have theological beliefs and in fact believe in God or a higher power, the two part ways very quickly when the question of acceptance, faith and the capacity of man is put into play. In a nutshell, the Universal/Natural worldview is a vision of understanding and accepting one's inferiority to the complexity of a vast universal dynamic where man is not at the center. While the Humanistic/Synthetic worldview is one which places the individual at the center of control and power without the acceptance of a vast unknown. The Humanistic/Synthetic is a worldview that sees man as superior and capable of creating dynamic change. While the Universal/Natural worldview recognizes that dynamic change within society is the result of a systemic process.

The terms used to describe the two worldviews are appropriate to simplify the discussion on theology. The names given to each worldview describes the fundamental perception of how the world operates. Is the locus of control and understanding of theology universal and natural or is it humanistic and synthetic? Some thoughts from others on this topic will expand on the theory and should help in explaining the concepts in greater detail.

Sydney Smith stated: "No man can ever end with being superior who will not begin with being inferior." While Malcolm Muggeridge concluded: "Human beings cannot live and operate in this world without some concept of a being greater them themselves, and of a purpose that transcends their own egotistic or greedy desires." Muggeridge went on to state: "Once you eliminate the notion of God, a creator, once you eliminate the notion that the creator has a purpose for us and that life consists essentially in fulfilling that purpose, then you are bound, as Pascal pointed out, 'To induce the megalomania of which we've seen so many manifestations in our time." Once again, we must be reminded of the behaviors of leaders like Mao or Stalin to serve as examples of Pascal's megalomania.

In applying the binary views of theology in which the Humanistic/Synthetic worldview place themselves at the center, Thomas Sowell made a forceful argument that explains their behavior in a modern context:

> Institutions that force-feed students the new trinity of race, class, and gender victimhood throughout the academic year are often unwilling to risk allowing even one lecture by a visiting spokesman for an opposing viewpoint. Like the Communist regimes which electronically jammed broadcasts from the Voice of America during the Cold War, the new academic totalitarians apparently fear lest their years-long propaganda efforts be knocked over like a house of cards by one brief exposure to a few facts and a different vision.

Morality also plays into the theological discussion. To the Universal/Natural mind human nature is evil and thus no individual can trust himself alone to be a good person alone without a spiritual underpinning because man alone is not powerful enough. The reason for this is because man is human and thus fallible to his nature. If a higher power is your frame of reference, one can become humble. It comes down to a matter of accepting and admitting your sinful nature and being guided by a spirit that is not fallible and will not act like a human with an inherently flawed will. For the Universal/Natural mind, moral control and power must come from an external spirit so that one can be guided to do what is right.

Counter to this perception of morality is the Humanistic/Synthetic mind that believes an individual can trust himself to be a moral person alone without a spiritual underpinning because man alone is powerful enough to do what is right without the incentives theology provides. The reason for this is a belief that human nature is good and man is thus only fallible if he is in an environment that is evil. One need not humble and subjugate to a higher power and thus need not accept and admit a sinful nature. As a result, moral control can be internal with power coming from an inner spirit that will not act with a flawed will. Because of this the individual with a Humanistic/Synthetic vision believe they will guide themselves to do what is right.

These comparisons may seem confusing when applied to each worldview. In fact the discussion of human nature outlined above is important enough that an entire chapter will be devoted to the topic. We must next look to some specifics of religion to outline a more precise picture of how the two worldviews relate religion to their perception of the world.

To the Universal/Natural vision, only God is omniscient/omnipotent (all knowing/all powerful) and completely good, nobody else, especially not humans. In effect, utopia is found in God's kingdom not on Earth. While the philosophy of the Humanistic/Synthetic behave and see the world from a personally omniscient/omnipotent position that allows them to believe they can engineer utopia on Earth. One could say that the Humanistic/Synthetic doctrine places itself on the same plane as God if they even believe in a power higher than self. There is a general lack of acceptance to the idea in the Humanistic/Synthetic vision that they as individuals are sinful or have an evil human nature. This perception is yet another aspect in psychological developmental where the Humanistic/Synthetic refuse to accept the fact or see the possibility that they are evil, or are capable of evil, or that others are capable of evil, or that sin has consequences beyond the here and now. The Humanistic/

Synthetic vision does not perceive that only through acceptance and submission to a power greater than humanity can one come to grips with the inhumanity of their behaviors and seek a road map to become a better person.

This mind set leads to moral relativity and secular humanism as a way of life for the Humanistic/Synthetic individual and thus theology plays a minor role in their lives. The Humanistic/Synthetic believe that whatever an individual defines as morally justifiable must be accepted because their approach to life is non religious and focused on the individual in the here and now. Because of this, the Humanistic/Synthetic feels no responsibility for acting in ways that respect others. In other words, there is a lack of understanding that there are other people riding on the bus.

The Universal/Natural vision sees man as evil, sinful and behaving out of self-interest. Thus it is necessary to believe in a power beyond that of an egocentric perspective to understand their humanity and follow a road set forth by a universal order or one who is completely good. This path is followed in order to attempt to be the best they can be so as to glorify and legitimize God's ultimate power by faith. Man is not omnipotent and thus does not have the ability to answer all of the unanswerable universal questions. Thus man must have faith in the unanswerable by acceptance of a power higher then self. The Universal/Natural accepts the role theology plays in their lives because human nature is sinful, and evil. Because of this, the Universal/Natural feels a responsibility for acting in ways that respect others. In other words, they understand that there are other people riding on the bus.

Fundamental to the understanding of worldviews is the developmental change that takes place as one goes from the Humanistic/Synthetic vision to the Universal/Natural vision. This key developmental stage takes place as one accepts one's "self" or moves towards self-actualization and realizes the insignificance of their humanity when weighed against the dynamics of the universe. When this is coupled with a genuine faith that offers solace, grace and forgiveness, those who ascribe to the Universal/Natural view find inner peace.

It is important to note that Abraham Maslow was the founder of Humanistic Psychology and the concept of self-actualization. Thus, it may seem at face value to be contradictory to the analysis at hand, but nothing could be farther from the truth. The Founding fathers have had their deist beliefs distorted by those who would like to rewrite history and say they were not men of God. In this same vain, the intelligentsia have turned Humanistic Psychology into a discipline counter to its base in an attempt to use it to legitimize the dogma of the Humanistic/Synthetic philosophy. The bottom line is that in order to become self actualized one must come to terms with the good, the bad and the ugly aspects of themselves. To do this, an individual must place oneself against the universal question of "why". The only possible way to deal with such a question, and thus find self-acceptance, is through a cognitive acceptance in a greater power or God. For example, becoming self actualized means searching for the answers to questions such as "why am I here", or "why do I have such opportunities", or "why did my best friend have to die so young". Since no human could possibly answer such questions, self-actualization can only be accomplished by acceptance in a universal power greater than self. This allows an individual to "let go" of the "self" they can't possibly come to terms with alone or through interaction with other humans.

This theory concerning theology thus begs the question that may be causing confusion within the critical mind. Why do those with a Universal/Natural doctrine believe that everyone is born evil because if God creates them why wouldn't they be good?

The Universal/Natural worldview would say that God gave man the capacity to be good if they followed a theological philosophy. They perceive that man is evil and will follow the natural laws that govern the universe of animals but also had the added ability to reason within this framework. This creates a situation that is consistent with natural law and at the same time allows for the ability for man to live and embrace the gift of reason they were given. In other words, man has the capacity to accept God or a higher power in order to move beyond a world guided by natural law. To summarize, there is something greater than self that created a set of universal moral laws and natural laws that apply and govern social systems allowing man to become civilized.

The Humanistic/Synthetic vision does not accept this analysis. They neglect the ability to reason beyond themselves and what they can see and just assume they are somehow better than the other animals in the kingdom. This perception is a self centered or egocentric worldview, which is contradictory to the Universal/Natural vision.

Lastly in our discussion of religion we must touch base with the concept of theology and violence. Neither worldview advocates violence, yet the Universal/Natural does accept that human nature is evil and violence will sometimes happen. What is key to this topic is that for the Universal/Natural world view one may die for their religion but one must not kill for their religion. For the Humanistic/Synthetic worldview one may allow killing for their secular religion, which might be called social justice, but one would never offer ones life for it.

Some final quotes will add to the discussion and thought process concerning theology. Basil Hume stated: "Moral choices do not depend on personal preference and private decision but on right reason and, I would add, divine order." While John Locke offered: "To give a man full knowledge of morality, I would send him to no other book than the New Testament."

Theology

Humanistic/Synthetic	Universal Natural
Scientific theory of theology	Religious theory of theology
Tempered by religion	Tempered by science
Determinism	Accepting of nature of universe
Mans role in universe is large	Predestination
Ability to master forces of nature	Humbled acceptance of God
Individual at center of control	Nature is center of control
Trinity: race, class, gender,	Holy trinity
Academic totalitarians	Inferior to vast natural dynamic
Can trust himself to overcome evil	Can't trust self w/o moral guidance
Human nature is good	Man is fallible—accept sinful nature
Environment is evil	External control
Internal control	God is omniscient
Omnipotent	Consequences beyond here and now
Moral relativity	
Secular humanism	
Ego-centric	

9

HUMAN NATURE

"The founders of a new colony, whatever Utopia of human virtue and happiness they might originally project, have invariably recognized it among their earliest practical necessities to allot a portion of the virgin soil as a cemetery, and another portion as the site of a prison."
—Nathaniel Hawthorne

Chapter 9 deals with the next piece of the developmental puzzle that helps to shape our worldviews. Human nature or the articulation of what human nature encompasses is a topic that is not rocket science, yet each world view has completely different definitions of what human nature is and how it operates within the behavior of individuals.

One of the first areas to explore in dealing with the topic of human nature focuses on the question, Is man good or evil? We have previously explored the theological ramifications of worldviews that cuts to the heart of this question but here we will look at good and evil from a different perspective.

Human nature to those with a Humanistic/Synthetic worldview is a negative aspect of man that has been created by evil institutions. In other words, mans nature is evil because institutions have made him that way. To the Humanistic/Synthetic mind a baby is born good; and if not corrupted by bad environmental influences, the child is capable of overcoming evil and doing what is right on their own without any external incentives. Thus, the behaviors of man in changing and engineering society can be trusted to be done in the best interest of man because man's nature is essentially good. In other

76

words the Humanistic/Synthetic have no fear in placing power in the hands of a few social engineers because they view them as intrinsically good.

Contrary to the Humanistic/Synthetic belief system is the view of human nature from the standpoint of the Universal/Natural worldview. In their view human nature is a negative aspect of man that is inherent in our genetic make-up and plays a vital role in the survival of man as a member of the kingdom of animals. In other words, man is evil because the laws of nature or natures God has made him that way in order to survive. To the Universal/Natural mind a baby is born evil and if not controlled by positive environmental influences, the child will not be capable of overcoming their negative nature to do what is right. Thus, the behaviors of man in changing and engineering society can not be trusted to be done in the best interest of man because mans nature is essentially evil and self serving. For this very reason the Universal/Natural are weary of placing power in the hands of a few to engineer society.

John Stewart Mill countered this perception. "Human nature is not a machine to be built after a model and set to do exactly the work prescribed for it, but a tree, which requires to grow and develop itself on all sides, according to the tendencies of the inward forces which make it a living thing." Francis Bacon added: "There is in human nature generally more of the fool than of the wise."

Many have pondered the question of human nature that will help to refine the Universal/Natural worldview. Hervey Allen summed up the Universal/Natural vision of human nature: "Each new generation is a fresh invasion of savages." Thomas Sowell added: "If you are not prepared to use force to defend civilization, then be prepared to accept barbarism. In short, the Universal/Natural view human nature as brutal and reason as beautiful, while the Humanistic/Synthetic view human nature as beautiful and reason as brutal.

One point needs to be clarified before continuing. Both visions understand that a positive environment is a necessity to promote the productive development of humans. The difference is that the Humanistic/Synthetic want to engineer the environment through the governmental institution while the Universal/Natural perceive a positive developmental environment as the outcome of systemic change created by the beneficial interplay of the social institutions. This concept will be discussed further in chapters 11-16.

The key to understating the difference is the perception of human nature between the two worldviews focuses in on an important question. Is man an animal working within the dynamic interplay of nature or is man a higher being who is not bound to the natural workings of the environment in which he has been placed? To the Universal/Natural vision there is an acceptance of man's narrow dominance in the animal kingdom because of his ability to reason. This is coupled with an understanding that natural forces act as a powerful motivation to guide man's behavior in evil ways in order to ensure his survival.

For those with a Humanistic/Synthetic vision, man is not on the same plane as the other animals in the kingdom and thus the forces that are at play within the animal world do not apply to man. Clearly man is above the other animals in the kingdom as far as reason goes, but the two visions apply this fact differently. The capacity to reason and do what is right within the context of understanding one's evil is much different than believing one will do what is right simply because it is assumed man is naturally good and above animal behavior. The former is a perception of the Universal/Natural worldview while the latter is a tenet of the Humanistic/Synthetic worldview.

In summary, human nature plays a vital role in the behavior of man for the Universal/Natural vision while it plays little to no role in the Humanistic/Synthetic vision. Larry P. Arnn details the differences in defining what role human nature plays to both the worldviews. He shows how powerful worldviews are in the public debate as well as in shaping social policy.

Arnn sees American society as being dominated by the Humanistic/Synthetic vision of human nature:

> According to it (Humanistic/Synthetic worldview), human nature is not fixed but evolves. Furthermore, this evolution comes to be something that we ourselves control. To believe that man can control his evolution is to believe in effect that we can create ourselves. We can take the place of God. This way of thinking comes to us from German Historicism, but in America it became known as Progressivism. Early in the last century it began to take over the academic world. Gradually it took over the Democratic Party and got a very powerful influence on the government.

Modern science in all its wonder faces important ethical questions in regard to what Arnn has articulated. An evolving human nature brings with it a belief in cloning, DNA manipulation and a volatile mixture of philosophies that support the claim that humans should not be burdened by their nature. These thoughts are exciting for the Humanistic/Synthetic and terrifying for the Universal/Natural.

In terms of human nature, the two worldviews perceive the concept of trusting man and his intentions in polar opposite ways. For the Universal/Natural mind, man is capable of good but one must never stray to far from the fact that man is capable of terrible acts of evil. In this vision, trust is connected with reason and historical fact. On the other hand, the Humanistic/Synthetic mind takes trust to the level of blind acceptance that man will do the right thing, even against the backdrop of history. In other words, the Humanistic/Synthetic would say trust me because I am good by nature, while the Universal/Natural would say I will trust you within reason because of human nature.

Thomas Sowell once again offers up a clear accounting of the differences between the two worldviews in terms of human nature, trust and reason. "The great curse of the 20th century was the inability of decent people to realize that what was unthinkable to them was both thinkable and doable by others—like Hitler, Stalin, Mao and Pol Pot." The Humanistic/Synthetic seem incapable of understanding the evil that lurks beneath the surface of human nature. It is this example of blind perceptions that has cost 170 million lives in the last century alone, not in war but by government decree. In the former USSR alone 65 million were killed while the government of the Peoples Republic of China slaughtered 35-40 million citizens.

This analysis alone does not fully explain the role human nature plays within the two worldviews. To offer up further insight into the role nature plays on man we must look at the teachings of Sigmund Freud. Before we delve into Freud's work it must be noted that it is not his literal wording and analysis that offers important insights; it is the symbolic cognitive processes and conceptual models he built that offers a unique understanding into human behavior. Remember, just because Freud uses what might be called absurd definitions and perverse situational descriptions, does not make the conceptual gains acquired by such terminology any less important.

Freud offered some important insights into the question of human natures' place in the behavior of individuals when he stated: "Men are more moral than they think and far more immoral than they can imagine." He also offered his feelings on the development of humans and civilization by saying: "The first human who hurled an insult instead of a stone was the founder of civilization." Clearly Freud was describing a perception of human nature that assumed man was evil yet capable of good, a belief consistent with the Universal/Natural worldview.

Freud's philosophy of human behavior and internal genetic cognitive motivation makes some key connections into the development of worldviews. Let's review some of the basic ideas Freud put forth and then use the theory to show how worldview development is effected. In simple terms, Freud described the human psyche as being comprised of three distinct behavioral guides.

The first is called the Id. This internal guide controls basic sexual and aggressive drives. It is the animalistic aspect of human behavior and functions for reasons of survival. The Id is what one might call the evil side of human nature. The second part is called the Super Ego. This internal guide can best be called our conscience. It is the area that allows man to have moral purity and the ability to understand right from wrong. The Super Ego offers the best in human potential and can be associated with mans nurturing side. The third part to Freud's analysis of the human condition is called the Ego. This internal guide for behavior can best be called the self. The self's role is to balance out the urges of the Id and Super Ego to create a individual that has the ability to operate within the framework of their evil human nature as well as show the capacity to move beyond self serving behaviors and understand right from wrong.

Now that we have defined Freud's theories we need to connect them to our discussion of worldview development. The Universal/Natural worldview may not be able to articulate Freud's theories. But they perceive the world from the standpoint that their Id is at play at all times and they must be ever weary of their capacity to act out on the impulses the Id drives them to fulfill. They have a more balanced sense of Ego as the interplay between their Id and Super Ego is accepted. Furthermore, the Universal/Natural worldview realizes that without an external incentive from institutional forces, including but not limited to a theological external locus of control, their Id will become dominant in their behaviors.

Those with a Humanistic/Synthetic worldview operate idealistically from their Super Ego without acceptance of their Id and its animal like nature. This blind and ideological self trust that ignores the Id allows them the freedom to believe that they have the capacity to figure out what is right without the need of having to deal with factoring the Id into the equation. This may sound nice as it seems those with the Humanistic/Synthetic world view behave from pure moral consciousness, but this is misleading and can cause problems with reasoned thought. The result of this perceptual reality is that the Humanistic/ Synthetic will undertake blind morally superior experiments in attempting to shape society that do not take into consideration man's basic desires of the Id. Because of this, assumptions are created in an idealistic form that are flawed from the start and are harmful to the survival of civilization.

There are other topics that relate to human nature that help to define one's worldview. Lets examine some of the fundamental perceptions of the Universal/Natural vision in order to define the differences between the two world visions. The Universal/Natural mind perceives man as being hard wired by DNA to survive and live according to the laws of nature, yet possessing the ability to reason in order to move beyond basic instincts. They understand the theory of homeostasis or the need to have balance in life on a dynamic planet. They accept that humans behave in ways to seek pleasure and avoid pain. In fact, John Locke said: "Good and evil, reward and punishment, are the only motives to a rational creature: these are the spur and reins whereby all mankind are set on work, and guided." Continuing our analysis, the Universal/Natural see humans as animals built to survive through strong drives including those which are nasty. They accept the fact that man is the meanest animal in the kingdom but also the most altruistic. They see that both the environment and DNA shape what we become. They accept that there are differences in all individuals and these differences are a part of natures plan to create diverse sets of DNA in order to protect the human species. They acknowledge however that these differences are minute in the whole of the human animal among a dynamic universal order. For example, certain people are immune to certain diseases. This protects the human gene pool if the disease were ever to become widespread always allowing some members of the human race to survive.

The debate over nature verses nurture in the development process and acquisition of worldviews also needs to be addressed at this time. Understanding the differences between the two views is a matter of degree and locus of control as to how large of a role nurture plays.

The Humanistic/Synthetic mind gives nurture a large role in explaining the outcomes of an individual life. What is defined as positive or negative life outcomes is the result of an external nurture that is beyond the control of the individual. DNA and human nature are not seen as prohibitive and thus are not a cause for negative life events or behaviors. Because of these perceptions, personal responsibility for behaviors and actions is not taken. In short, problems are caused by an external nurture that if controlled can be made to be perfectible. This is why the Humanistic/Synthetic view the behavior of criminals as caused by evil social institutions, not the individuals themselves. In short, restaurants that serve hot coffee are responsible for the burns caused as a result of a customer spilling the coffee on their lap.

Contrasting these arguments, the Universal/Natural worldview gives nurture a balanced role in explaining the outcomes of an individual life. What is defined as a positive or negative life event or behavior is the result of both an external nurture and internal DNA that work together to create particular life outcomes for an individual. Negative life events or behaviors are not blamed on external institutional influences that are beyond the control of the individual. DNA and human nature have the potential to be prohibitive or negative but personal responsibility for behaviors and actions is taken. In short, problems caused by an internal nature can be controlled to create the best possible outcomes. While at the same time, external negative nurture is accepted and dealt with through personal growth. In short, the Universal/Natural accepts the fact that if one drops hot coffee on there lap, it is not the fault of the fast food restaurant.

In closing, Ludwig Von Mises leaves us with a quote that seems appropriate to the discussion in defining the difference each world view holds in regard to human nature. "Human civilization is not something achieved against nature; it is rather the outcome of the working of the innate qualities of man."

Human Nature

Humanistic/Synthetic	Universal/Natural
Institutions are evil	Man is evil
Man is basically good	Man is self-serving
Engineer society	Man is an animal with reason
Man separate from other animals	Human nature plays vital role
Human nature plays minor role	Human nature is fixed
Human nature evolves	Trust based on reason/ historical fact
Historicism	Realize the unthinkable in others
Progressivism	Id is ignored/tempered by superego
Trust: acceptance that man will do right	Control by institutional forces
View some behaviors as unthinkable	Homeostasis
Super Ego is dominant	Humans seek pleasure/ avoid pain
Id is ignored	Man is meanest animal
Blind morally superior experiments	Environment and DNA shape man
Idealistic	Individuals have differences
Nurture plays a larger role	Personal responsibility
Blame the environment	Man is altruistic animal

10

NATURE

"The mastery of nature is vainly believed to be an adequate substitute for self mastery."—Reinhold Niebuhr

The next topic deals with man's perception of nature and his role in the environment. As you would suspect by this time the two worldviews take entirely differing views when it comes to nature. Both worldviews understand the dynamic interplay that nature has on the world and yet the two see man's role from opposite perspectives. The questions we need to ask include. Are humans a part of nature? What role does environmentalism play within the two worldviews? Should man try to override nature? Finally, we need to look at the question of creationism and evolution to clear up some confusing philosophical questions.

No one argues that nature plays a vital role in shaping man's world but the two worldviews apply their differing perspectives on nature in stark contrast. The Universal/Natural mind views nature as something that can't be tamed or overcome. Nature is seen as something to work with not against. There is an acceptance of the grand scheme of nature and a respect for its power and complexity. The Universal/Natural worldview sets limits on how far man should go in his advancement to circumvent natural laws and is always mindful of working within the framework that nature provides. In short, an ethical component is tied to working with nature.

An old television commercial comes to mind to make this point. Back in the 60's there was a Parkay margarine ad that showed a crowned woman who represented Mother Nature. She tasted the Parkay margarine and because it tasted like butter the sounds of lightning were heard as she said in a stern voice, "It's not nice to fool Mother Nature." The Universal/Natural vision would agree with this commercial. Not that they are against margarine, but that even though man can build things that override nature they must be very wary of the long term consequences of their actions. In other words, man may be able to fly to the moon, build homes on the beach or clone sheep but that does not mean space ships will not explode, homes will not be lost to hurricanes and cloning sheep will not cause unforeseen consequences.

The Universal/Natural mind views natural laws as something to respect and they connect this same mind set to the laws of nature as they apply to man. As previously detailed, the understanding that there are universal laws that transcend man is a fundamental principal within the Universal/Natural worldview. They, unlike their counter view, see man's role with nature as one of co-existence where man is every part as much of the natural order of things as any other animal or natural process. They are not ashamed of man's role in the world or his right to live and act in ways to build, produce and consume, yet cautious of the ramifications of their actions.

Lao-Tzu exemplified the Universal/Natural vision as it applies to the environment:

> Nothing in the world is more flexible and yielding than water. Yet when it attacks the firm and the strong, none can withstand it, because they have no way to change it. So the flexible overcome the adamant, the yielding overcome the forceful. Everyone knows this, but no one can do it.

On the other end of world perspectives is the Humanistic/Synthetic view of nature. According to this vision, nature is something that can be tamed and overpowered. There is not a general acceptance of the grand scheme of nature and a respect for its power and complexity. Nature is seen as something to be mastered. In fact, John Adams asked an important question concerning man controlling nature: "The question before the human race is whether the God of nature shall govern the world by his own laws, or whether priests and kings shall rule it by fictitious miracles." The Humanistic/Synthetic world view does not set limits on how far man should go in his advancements to circumvent nature's laws and is not always mindful of working within the framework that nature provides. In short, ethics plays a limited role in working with nature.

The Humanistic/Synthetic mind views the environment with awe and yet does not give the same respect to the laws of nature as they apply to man. As previously seen, the understanding that there are universal laws that transcend man is not a fundamental principal within their worldview. They however unlike their counter view see man's role with nature as one of reckless destruction of the environment. In their view man is to play no part in the natural order of things. The Humanistic/Synthetic are ashamed of man's role in the environment and his right to live and act in ways that use, build, produce and consume.

This may all seem counter to what you have been led to believe as those with the Humanistic/Synthetic worldview act as if they champion environmental causes alone. The truth is that those with a Humanistic/Synthetic vision act in ways that counter the unknown powers of natural law without reflection as to the consequences of their actions on the grand scheme of the universe. This point offers the opportunity to present a simple explanation to see how words and actions are often at odds in the Humanistic/Synthetic worldview. The current dogma of the left is that they alone care about the environment and yet their world perception of utopian engineering is counter to a belief in accepting the dynamics of the environment within the context of the laws of nature. Some call this intellectual inconsistency, others call it hypocrisy to pretend to be what one is not.

Technology is seen by the Humanistic/Synthetic worldview as something that can master nature and its associated laws because there is not an acceptance to a greater order and a humbling of self within the context of universal laws. The focus for the Humanistic/Synthetic is on self and the ability to change and engineer society in a way that they see as correct, even if the fabric created goes against all that we do not understand. Remember, "it's not nice to fool Mother Nature."

For the Universal/Natural mind, technology has limits within natural laws where ethical and philosophical questions are to be revered and respected.

An example will help to explain the difference in perception of mans place in nature. The truth to this next tale may be questionable but it does not matter as much as the symbolic metaphor it represents.

According to the story, a young seal near death was found caked in oil after the Exxon Valdez disaster in Alaska. After months of rehabilitation the seal was taken back to its habitat to be released with much fanfare and media attention. As the seal was released into the water and the crowd roared with applause and cheers, a killer whale swam up, captured the seal in its mouth and proceeded to devour the seal. The story in itself is not the true explanation of the difference between the two worldviews. It was the reaction to the event that sets up our explanation. At the sighting of the seal being swallowed up, those with a Humanistic/Synthetic worldview gasped with despair and anguish. While those with the Universal/Natural worldview saw the event as nothing more than nature with all its brutality and beauty as well as the futility of changing its course.

Another example showing the differences between the two worldviews can be seen by contrasting the perceptions given to beavers in their natural habitat. The Humanistic/Synthetic worldview has no problem with beavers cutting down trees, damning rivers and altering the flow of streams with the death of many other animals as a result. However, they do have a problem if man cuts down trees, damns rivers and alters the flow of streams with the death of many other animals as a result. Clearly, one vision, the Universal/Natural, places man as a part of the environment while the other places man outside the environment.

This is not a problem for the Universal/Natural world view because they do not believe that man, being just one animal in the vast kingdom, has the power to have much effect on the overall environment and all of its complexity. The Humanistic/Synthetic vision however does believe it has the power to control the dynamic nature of the universe. The issue of global warming can be used to exemplify the point. In the Humanistic/Synthetic vision man has the power and is in fact causing global warming. The Universal/Natural vision would think it arrogant to believe that man has the power to alter the dynamics of an Earth they know little about and have barely, in relative terms, lived upon.

If we were to associate the Humanistic/Synthetic analysis of man's role on nature to other natural events that have occurred on a grand scale, one would then have to blame dinosaurs for the ice age because they were the dominant creatures during their time. In addition, moral pronouncements from the Humanistic Synthetic advocating Earth Day celebrations provide a telling example of their confusion regarding man and the environment. Thomas Sowell has pointed out, "The next time you hear an alarming speech about "global warming" on Earth Day, just remember that the first Earth Day featured alarms about the danger of a new ice age."

Next we will look at the question of Evolution versus Creationism from both schools of thought. No discussion of nature would be complete if nature's role concerning evolution and natural selection were not addressed. The first and most fundamental problem is pitting these two theories of man's existence against one another.

It is not difficult for the Universal/Natural worldview to formulate the idea that a higher order or God created the world and thus fully subscribe to the theory of Creationism. At the same time, the Universal/Natural vision accepts through reason and scientific facts, that evolution has occurred to the animals of the world, including man. Thus, the theories are not separate as the Humanistic/Synthetic mind would have you believe but they coincide. The theories are aligned because a higher power or God created the natural components of the Earth, including natural selection, that man inhabits and is a integral part of.

James Q. Wilson adds to the explanation regarding the question concerning man and natural selection:

> Man is a social animal who struggles to reconcile the partially warring parts of his universally occurring nature—the desire for survival and sustenance with the desire for companionship and approval. And not just a social animal by accident, but a social animal by nature—that is, as the consequence of biological predisposition's selected over eons of evolutionary history.

Because of the secular nature of the Humanistic/Synthetic vision, the theories of Evolution and Creationism must be kept separate. For the Humanistic/Synthetic it becomes a matter of what one can see versus what one cannot. If it cannot be seen or verified, it must be rejected. This can be done in the Humanistic/Synthetic mind because their perspective operates with cognitive impunity and disconnects from any ramifications associated with what can't be seen or what they do not understand. As a result, Evolution is held on sacred ground while Creationism is disregarded as hack intellectualism.

The question concerning the evolution of human nature must also be addressed at this point. For the Humanistic/Synthetic, human nature evolves and is perfectible by the use of power by the state to socially engineer man. In other words, mans negative nature can be eliminated. This is not a natural evolutionary process in the sense of what Darwin has detailed. The irony here is that the Humanistic/Synthetic worldview holds evolutionary theory as a cornerstone and yet feels the need to ignore its principles and supplant natural law with man as the evolutionary engineer. In fact, Charles Darwin stated: "The evolution of the human race will not be accomplished in the ten thousand years of tame animals, but in the million years of wild animals, because man is and will always be a wild animal."

As previously discussed, the Universal/Natural worldview accepts human nature as a part of man that will always exist, even if it evolves in the sense that evolutionary theory outlines. The Universal/Natural mind views a human nature that is not perfectible. Although man's nature may evolve as a result of natural selection, man has and will always be directed by his nature. In other words, man's negative nature will never be eliminated as it acts in ways to assure his survival.

Finally, natural law offers us the theory of cycles. The premise is that the Universe works in a cyclical fashion. For example, cycles can be found in light waves, electricity or the equal and opposite reactions seen in physics. These cycles, like waves upon the oceans, act and result in an Earth that is in balance at all times. Humans call the phenomena the yin and yang, or say when things are bad that they can only get better. Even the stock market and business climate work in cycles and sadly enough, some say when you are in love every good day will be balanced out with a bad one. Most of the time the cycles work in a predictable manner, but there are times when the cycle undulates wildly and crashes occur or miracles happen.

For example, the stock market crash of 1929, nasty divorces, or a miracle that sustains a life beyond the science of medicine clearly shows the highs and lows of human cycles. The importance of the application of cycle theory to worldviews is significant. The Humanistic/Synthetic worldview of social engineering by default has a higher potentiality to create crashes and believes it has the ability to engineer miracles. Metaphorically speaking however, the good intentions of Dr. Frankenstein to engineer a superior life form lead to monstrous results. On the other hand, the Universal/Natural has faith in the relative size and frequency of cycles and thus there is less possibility of engineering society into a crash. As far as miracles are concerned, the Universal/Natural accepts their possibility and rejoices upon their arrival.

The perception understands a stable balanced world is fundamental not only in nature but within themselves. They accept the cycle theory and apply it to their lives. Individual balance is achieved through a physiological process called homeostasis, and a cognitive process of self-acceptance. As a result the Universal/Natural never take themselves to seriously or place too much emphasis on day to day happenings that they have no ability to control individually. Theirs is a proactive vision of working within the confines of a cyclical universe. As a result there is a sense of humor associated with life and a belief that the society is greater than the individual but it is the whole of individuals in society that causes systemic social change over time.

In contrast, the Humanistic/Synthetic worldview is based on emotion and thus disregards the aforementioned cycle theory. It is a vision that is based on internal turmoil and is thus reactionary and unstable. The approach to life is less associated with a sense of humor and more focused on self-defined intellectual superiority with outrage expressed towards those who do not agree with their views. They see the individual as greater than the whole of society in determining social change.

Clearly both worldviews are at odds when articulating and acting upon their unique perceptual framework of nature. Unfortunately, the misapplication of worldviews between man and his environment can result in unforeseen consequences that can be and have been a matter of life and death.

Nature

Humanistic/Synthetic	Universal/Natural
Nature can be tamed and mastered	Nature can't be tamed
Man is outside of nature	Respect for nature's power
Man is negative influence to nature	Ethical limits on influencing nature
Remove man's environmental influence	Co-existence
Technology can master nature	Man is a part of the environment
Shocked by natures brutality	Accepts natures beauty/brutality
Man is outside of environment	Technology involves ethics
Man has powerful over environment	Creationism and Evolution
Creationism and Evolution kept separate	Focus on what we can and can't see
Evolution is focus	World is stable and balanced
Focus on what one can see	Do not take life to seriously
Emotional	Proactive vision
Internal turmoil	Sense of humor
Reactionary	Express acceptance
Less balanced	The whole of decisions cause change
Self defined intellectuals	Cycles are varied
Engineer crashes/create miracles	Accept miracles

III

APPLICATION

A systemic process of human growth and cognitive development creates a perceptual worldview in humans that aligns with two distinct models. This development is constructed through individual cognitive growth in several areas. These areas include the formation, perception and formulation or personal expression of the workings of morality, needs, learning, power, leadership, theology, human nature and nature. These developmental areas become the matrix for underscoring man's sequential progression of worldview formation that is binary in nature. The timing of growth in formulating one's worldview is determined by genetic temperament to a small degree and by environmental influences in a larger sense; with the acquisition of a Humanistic/Synthetic vision proceeding that of the Universal/Natural. This sequence is predictable but not automatic because growth into a Universal/Natural worldview is ultimately a process only an individual can undertake. For many, this personal struggle is avoided either because of a lack of effort or because environmental influences have created a cognitive framework that is unable too fully develop and thus perceive the world from the Universal/Natural perspective.

Now that the developmental patterns, perceptions and assumptions that form one's worldview have been detailed, it is necessary to discuss how an individual will express their vision within the greater society in which they live. In order to see how worldviews are applied, part three will discuss how each worldview functions within the context of the five institutions that make up a civilization. As previously outlined in chapter 2, the application of one's worldview towards the proper functioning of the institutions that make up our society is a vital issue for its health and continued success. Let us then move forward with a critical mind and the ability to analyze what we are thinking so that we can clearly see what is successful and/or detrimental to our social structure.

11

INSTITUTIONS AND CIVILIZATION

"The less a person knows about the workings of the social institutions of his society, the more he must trust those who wield power in it; and the more he trusts those who wields such power, the more vulnerable he makes himself to becoming their victim."—Thomas S. Szasz

If we are to apply each worldview to their particular perception on how society should function, we first need to look at what makes up a civilized society. Webster's Dictionary defines civilization in these terms: "to bring or come out of a primitive or savage condition to a higher level of social organization and of cultural and scientific development or; the total of a peoples culture where they have reached a high level of social development."

In order then to attain a higher level of cultural and social development necessary for civilization, a culture must have five particular institutions functioning independently yet working together towards positive cultural development. The five necessary institutions that make up a civilization are government, economic, education, family, and religion. Together they create the foundation that allows modern society to function with a higher level of social and cultural development because they offer the mechanisms to control and guide man away from barbaric instincts.

If any of the five institutions are weakened or lost, the civilization will suffer and digress at best or at worst die out. The Roman Empire is a good example of how institutional collapse can create conditions that will eventually lead to the downfall of civilized society. It is important to note that the Collapse of the Roman Empire occurred quietly over time, as the citizens were unaware of the environmental changes that were taking place within their society until it was too late.

Institutional decline does not occur in any set pattern with one specific institution preceding the others. The erosion may begin in any of the five fundamental pillars of civilized society or in unison. What is important to note is that once one institution begins to show weakness the other institutions are at risk. The primary signal however that institutional decline is underway can best be seen as one institution becomes dominant over the others. This shift in the balance of power begins a cycle of abuse where the dominant institution becomes involved in dictating the actions and redefining the principles of another institution. When this begins, the root causes for the collapse of civilization has taken hold.

The purpose of each institution is important for each plays a vital role in the health and vigor of the society. Webster's Dictionary helps define each institution in a limited way. Because of this, an expanded definition will be detailed so that the purpose of the institutions in the context of civilization will be clear.

First, the governmental institution is for the exercise of authority over a state in order to rule or control the people. The necessity for government is seen as people join into groups that need rules in order to control self-interest so the group can survive.

Second, the economic institution is for the management and satisfaction of the material needs of the people most notably the production, distribution and consumption of goods and services. The necessity for an economic system is seen as people join into groups that need to satisfy unlimited wants with limited resources in order to economize so the group can survive.

Third, the education institution is for developing the knowledge, skill or character training in a formal setting separate from the family but in concert. The necessity for education is seen as people join into groups that need to share information and skills in order to pass on vital learning and advance technology so the group can survive.

Forth, the family institution is for the procreation, nurture and establishment of nuclear groups of parents, children and relatives descended from a common ancestor or lineage. The necessity for the family institution is seen as people join into larger groups that need specifically defined sub groups in order to control development and nurture of the young so the group can survive.

Fifth, the religious institution is for the articulation and application of a specific system of belief in God or gods that includes worship often involving a code of ethics. The necessity for religion is seen as people join into groups that seek answers to the unanswerable questions in order to develop moral control and direct reasoned curiosity so the group can survive.

Civilization was a result of man joining into agriculturally based communities, turning away from the hunting and gathering cultures that preceded what one would call civilization. When man learned how to farm and domesticate animals it allowed him to settle into a larger social order and begin to form specialization of tasks. Social institutions were less important and defined under a "hunting and gathering" way of life that was controlled more by instinct and human nature. These institutions however became vitally important for order and success under a culture of sedentary agriculture in order to tame man's nature and create the social order necessary for survival.

A civilized society was beneficial because of the inherent advantages of living within a larger community where food was more plentiful and predictable. Time could be spent on other pursuits and specialized behaviors that would enable man to develop tools and strategies that would offer an advantage over those who had not joined together in a civilized society.

In effect, when man decided to take the route of building a community, he knowingly or not, agreed to the necessity to incorporate the social institutions into the culture. Ignoring the incorporation of the five institutions of civilized living would create a situation where hunting and gathering offered a greater chance of survival. Thus, the incentives created by forming an agrarian society had a cost, that being the necessity of forming and incorporating the five social institutions into the culture.

The question we are then faced with is how does each worldview define how the institutions should operate within the framework of modern society? Each worldview may accept the notion that the institutions are needed to survive but each gives differing weights of importance to the individual institutions.

The Universal/Natural worldview perceives the five institutions as equally important with each standing alone as pillars of their respective roles in the context of civilization. The Universal/Natural worldview offers respect to each institution and applies identical principles to each pillar understanding that the institutions must work independently and yet within the spirit of cooperation if the civilization is to thrive. One institution should not dominate nor should the role or power be unchecked as each plays a dynamic role in the success or failure of the civilization.

The Universal/Natural man accepts the reasoning that in order to have a civilized society man must be tamed by the institutions found therein. In other words the institutions provide incentives for man to behave in a civilized fashion. The institutions set up limited ground rules for civilized living (the "Can I" or written law) and create incentives to behave in ways that best advance the society (the Should I). The balance between the specific written laws ("Can I") will balance out the institutional incentives that create individual decisions beneficial to the advancement of the civilization ("Should I").

Institutional incentives that produce predictable behaviors are the cornerstone of civilized living. The government provides incentives by sending signals to individuals: "Follow the law or go to jail." The economy provides incentives by sending signals to individuals: "If you spend your money here you lost the opportunity to spend it elsewhere." The family provides incentives by sending signals to individuals: "Do not talk to strangers." Education provides incentives by sending signals: "Earning a degree will offer increased opportunities." Lastly, religion provides incentives by sending signals: "You will be held accountable for your sins."

Conversely, the Humanistic/Synthetic worldview sees the institutions as the reason for problems within the society and seeks to allow one institution to dominate the others in order to rid the culture of its poisonous elements. The Humanistic/Synthetic view of civilization is a doctrine that blames the institutions for the ills of society and not the nature of individuals. The irony is that the Humanistic/Synthetic worldview dismisses the fact that individuals are the ones creating the very institutions that they insist are the cause of the problems in society.

As a result, the Humanistic/Synthetic vision feels that man can civilize himself outside a framework of shared social institutions if one institution is given the power to engineer and mandate the proper way of living that they define as civilized. In other words, the "Can I" determine all of the "Should I". The fundamental institution of importance for the Humanistic/Synthetic worldview is, by default of the perception, the government institution. Take one look at America today and you will see how the governmental institution has become intrusive into every aspect of American life. Our limited constitutional government is now mandating behavior and values that were once the sole responsibility of the other institutions. Today, the government, through laws and judicial activism, is highly involved in the economy, runs the education system, disregards the family and strong arms religion and worship. Clearly, the government is attempting to determine the "Can I".

Both worldviews differ in their beliefs in the ability to have a utopian society. The Humanistic/Synthetic vision believes utopia can be reached if man is guided to perfection by governmental institutional control while the Universal/Natural worldview accepts the notion that man can only create a best case scenario based on his inherent limits, which is most certainly not a utopia. Positive social change for the Universal/Natural is the result of a systemic process that evolves as institutions provide incentives for man to freely make choices that have inherent costs.

In theory for the Humanistic/Synthetic believer, man can create utopia if all of the "Should I" were figured out and written down as law ("Can I") for all to follow perfectly. Conversely, the Universal/Natural vision would in theory create utopia if all of the "Should I" were adhered to by every human with perfection outside and circumventing any need for written laws ("Can I"). A utopian theory is feasible in the minds of the Humanistic/Synthetic worldview while it is something of a theoretical fantasy for those with the Universal/Natural worldview. It is no wonder those with the idealistic Humanistic/Synthetic worldview are quick to concentrate power in the governmental institution in hopes of creating what their minds can envision. In contrast, those with a Universal/Natural vision are more pragmatic and accepting in the reality of practice, trade offs, and systemic change, not the hope of rose colored theory.

To further exemplify this point, Thomas Sowell outlines the importance of the incentives that each institution offers:

> Cultures contain many cues and inducements to dissuade the individual from approaching ultimate limits, in much the same way that a special warning strip of land around the edge of a baseball field lets a player know that he is about to run into a concrete wall when he is preoccupied with catching the ball. The wider that strip of land and the more sensitive the player is to the changing composition of the ground under his feet as he pursues the ball, the more effective the warning. Romanticizing or lionizing as individualistic those people who disregard social cues and inducements increases the danger of head-on collisions with inherent social limits. Decrying various forms of social disapproval is in effect narrowing the warning strip.

In essence, Sowell is saying that the Universal/Natural worldview accepts the cultural constraints that the five social institutions provide in keeping civilization pointed in the right direction. The Humanistic/Synthetic worldview does not recognize the limits of man and thus ignores the signals that hold man in check and protect the shaky ground civilization rests upon.

This is not to say that the institutions are without fallibility. In fact, the institutions that men must create carry with them the ability to produce the collapse of the civilization they are trying to protect. William R. Inge warned us: "Every institution not only carries within it the seeds of its own dissolution, but prepares the way for its most hated rival." How this concept is respected by each worldview is important because the Universal/Natural worldview honors the inherent danger of institutional power while the Humanistic/Synthetic does not. In short, the Humanistic/Synthetic vision lives in a perceptual mindset that manifests itself in behaviors that create conditions that destroy the civilization unbeknownst to them. They do this because the vision does not see the potential evil in the governmental institution they have looked to empower to create the utopian society they dream of manufacturing.

Thus, an important component in the survival of a civilized culture is the ability to set limits and create checks and balances in and between each institution. The Universal/Natural worldview believes this as a fundamental necessity in the creation of a functional society while the Humanistic/Synthetic worldview does not. Chateubriand echoed the need for checks and balances between institutions: "Every institution goes through three stages—utility, privilege, and abuse".

The Splinter Theory will serve as an example of how the two worldviews apply institutional control over society. If one gets a splinter in their finger they have numerous institutional solutions as to how to remedy the problem.

For those with the Universal/Natural worldview each institution has advantages in splinter removal. The education institution would offer learning to the individual that would show how to remove the splinter, bandage it and allow it to heal. The family institution would provide help from mom and dad in removing the splinter, bandaging it and offering love, support and comfort. The religious institution would allow for prayer and strength in accepting the problem with the faith that getting a splinter is a part of life. The economic institution would offer the chance in developing a new and improved splinter remover. This would not only solve the problem but it would give the inventor the chance to market the remover, sell it and thus make a profit. Lastly, the government institution could pass legislation against the cause of the splinter and offer judicial remedies for pain and suffering.

For the Universal/Natural mind all of these solutions are equal in remedying the problem. Although each solution may have merit, the application will depend on the cost and benefit of each possible solution as well as the amount of personal responsibility the splinter holder possesses. The key in the decision to solve the problem of the splinter is up to the individual who may use one or more of the institutions to solve the problem. The answer will be a matter of balancing the "Can I" and "Should I".

A different application to the Splinter Theory would be used by the Humanistic/Synthetic worldview. This view does not hold each remedy as equal and important but sees the governmental institution as the most important problem solver. The blame for the splinter would be external and thus the splinter holder would look to the government to step in and solve the problem. The government of the Humanistic/Synthetic worldview would be quick to offer new legislation to solve the problem of splinters as well as evoke judicial remedies for pain and suffering. The Humanistic/Synthetic would not look to the education institution as they see it as a tool they use to control the worldview of students. They would not look to the family institution for they see it as an affront to their perception of personal choice and freedom. They would not look to the religious institution as they see it as theoretical and incapable of offering much help. They would not look to the economic institution as they see it as a powerful corporate scheme that only looks to take peoples money by controlling and dominating the marketplace.

The Splinter Theory clearly demonstrates the vast difference in how the two worldviews perceive the role of the five fundamental social institutions. The Humanistic/Synthetic sees the governmental institution as a means to an end they believe they can engineer regardless of the costs involved. The Universal/Natural views the institutions as a necessary means to an end, that being a civilized society. The Universal/Natural understand the important role each institution plays in creating civility and solving problems. This is tempered by the knowledge that institutions must work on an equal plane acting independently and interdependently. The Universal/Natural vision believes that if one institution gains too much power over the others, the decline of civilization will begin.

Both worldviews are sincere and want to have the best possible society in which to live. The Humanistic/Synthetic vision believe they can create a utopian society by centering power in the hands of the government moving further and further left on the political spectrum. This is fine in theory but practice has shown that to achieve utopia by moving to the political left society must first suffer the likes of institutions like democratic socialism, socialism, medieval mercantilism, feudalism, and communism. Clearly these experiments to move toward a theoretical utopia have failed miserably. In fact, social engineering experiments by Stalin, Mao, and Hitler cost over 50 million lives in the last century alone.

Fear of mass loss of life and personal freedom guides the Universal/Natural to an understanding that improving society is not a game and utopian ideals are nothing more than pipe dreams. The embrace of principles found within a democratic federal republic and the dynamics of systemic change offer the Universal/Natural mind the best case scenario between social engineering experiments of the far left and anarchy on the far right.

There are many examples over the course of history where one institution gained too much power or lost its equal station among the others. Roman governmental control, medieval religious control, Educational stagnation in ancient China, Communist economic control in the former Soviet Union and family decline currently underway in the United States are all examples of institutional misalignment that caused the decline or collapse of civilization.

Clearly, worldviews have had and will continue to have a profound impact on our civilization. Chapters 12-16 will examine the specifics of how each worldview relates to the five social institutions and discuss the ramifications of these beliefs on our social fabric.

The diversity of thought between the two worldviews as it relates to the functioning of the five social institutions is extensive. Because of this, the focus in the following chapters will be on some of the most pressing differences. The analysis will allow the reader to understand the application of how his or her worldview affects society. The outcome of this exercise will hopefully offer the ability for the reader to better articulate what it is that they believe and then contemplate the ramifications of their individual worldview on society.

Institutions and Civilization

Humanistic/Synthetic	Universal/Natural
Institutions cause problems in society	Institutions are pillars of civilization
Government institution dominates	Institutions are equal
"Can I" determines "Should I"	"Can I" and "Should I"
Believe in creating utopia	Apply = principles to each Institution
Utopia = all "Can I" articulated	No utopia only best case scenario
Work in theory	Theoretical utopia = all "Should I""
Institutions—not warning track	Institutions = warning track
Gov. institution is a means to an end	Power of institutions is checked/limited
Socialism	Man is tamed by institutions
Medieval mercantilism	Institutional incentives to act civil
Feudalism	Work in practice-trade offs/systemic
Communism	Accept ultimate limits
	Institutions are fallible

12

GOVERNMENT

"Any government is in itself an evil insofar as it carries within it the tendency to deteriorate into tyranny."—Albert Einstein

Government is a social institution built to control man by offering a set of rules and consequences in order for man to advance within a civil society. Each worldview understands the necessity of government but applies divergent attitudes as to how government should operate. Alexander Hamilton reminds us of the necessity to have a functioning government if we are to live in a civilized society. "Why has government been instituted at all? Because the passions of men will not conform to the dictates of reason and justice without constraint."

As we have already outlined, government is seen as the pivotal institution to those with a Humanistic/Synthetic worldview and a necessary evil to those with a Universal/Natural focus. James Madison added:

> What is government itself but the greatest reflections on human nature? If men were angels, no government would be necessary. If angels were to govern men, neither external nor internal controls on government would be necessary.

To better substantiate these differences we will begin by narrowing in on the five key principles that underscore our American Constitution. The concepts that offered by the founding fathers of this nation to guide our system of government include popular sovereignty, limited government, separation of powers, federalism, and civil rights/liberties. The definitions of these principles will set the stage for further analysis.

1. Popular sovereignty: The people have ultimate authority within our republic or representative democracy to elect representatives under a social contract. This social contract is an agreement that the people by consent will follow governmental rules as long as the government governs justly. Popular sovereignty applied means that government is by the consent of the governed. Aristotle understood this principle: "There are two parts of good government, one is the actual obedience of citizens to the laws, the other part is the goodness of the laws which they obey."

2. Limited government: The government will operate under a written constitution that is specific and bound by defined parameters that applies the law equally to every member of the society. John Adams called it: "A government of laws and not of men."

3. Separation of powers: The government will divide powers among several branches; legislative—make laws, executive—enforce laws and judicial—interpret laws; so that each can check and balance out the others in order to not allow one branch or individual to become too powerful. Montesquieu said: "Every man invested with power is apt to abuse it...To prevent this abuse, it is necessary from the very nature of things that power should be a check to power."

4. Federalism: A system of government that balances power between the state governments and federal government so as to further counteract any possibility of total control at the national level. The words of James Madison show the focus of the Founders. "The powers delegated by the proposed Constitution to the federal government are few and defined. Those which are to remain in the State governments are numerous and indefinite."

5. Civil rights/liberties: Defined unalienable rights are given to all individuals in society that transcend and are beyond the scope and power of the government. Alexander Hamilton said: "The sacred rights of mankind are not to be rummaged for among old parchments or musty records. They are written, as with a sunbeam, in the whole volume of human nature, by the hand of the divinity itself, and can never be obscured by mortal power."

Now that we have defined the principles that make up our system of governance we must look at how each worldview applies these principles to the functioning of government. If two words were used to describe the differences between the Universal/Natural worldview of government and the Humanistic/Synthetic, they would be limited versus unlimited.

The Humanistic/Synthetic vision uses the governmental institution to give ultimate authority to representatives who they deem as being superior at decision making. The vision holds the perception that the masses are not as capable of decision-making and believe the government is a tool necessary for social design.

For the Humanistic/Synthetic the principle of limited government is counter to any and all policy decisions they deem necessary and appropriate. Separation of powers is seen not as a tool for counteracting tyranny and unchecked power but a means to manipulate the institution to get the results they want. Federalism is used only if it can offer results to their agenda but is largely ignored and manipulated by using the power of the national government to circumvent the power of the states through fiscal blackmail. Lastly, civil rights and liberties are seen as not something beyond the control and scope of the government but as something the government gives to individuals through legislation and judicial activism. Thomas Jefferson exposed the problem of an unchecked judiciary however when he said: "The Constitution…is a mere thing of wax in the hands of the judiciary, which they may twist and shape into any form they please." Today, the judicial branch has become a tool the Humanistic/Synthetic vision uses to legislate their utopian agenda from the bench when statesmen representing the will of the people deny their policy agenda in the House and Senate.

Additionally, it should be noted that the Humanistic/Synthetic misinterpret the "Necessary and Proper" as well as the "General Welfare" statements of our limited government to loosely interpret the Constitution so it can be manipulated to fit their needs. The Universal/Natural use a strict interpretation of the Constitution. They define the "Necessary and Proper" clause to mean any new legislation must be specifically connected with powers already stated in the Constitution. In dealing with the specifics of constitutional interpretation, Thomas Jefferson said: "Congress has not unlimited powers to provide for the general welfare, but only those specifically enumerated." While James Madison, the father of the Constitution said: "With respect to the two words 'general welfare, I have always regarded them as qualified by the detail of powers connected with them. To take them in a literal and unlimited sense would be a metamorphosis of the Constitution into which there is a host of proofs was not contemplated by its creators."

T.S. Eliot may have articulated perhaps the best observation applicable to the Humanistic/Synthetic perception of the role of government in creating an engineered society:

> Half the harm that is done in this world is due to people who want to feel important. They don't mean to do harm—but the harm does not interest them. Or they do not see it, or they justify it because they are absorbed in the endless struggle to think well of themselves.

As you might guess the Universal/Natural worldview perceives the role of the governmental institution in ways that run counter to the Humanistic/Synthetic view. The Universal/Natural vision perceives the governmental institution as a result of the ultimate authority the people hold to elect representatives to facilitate the decision making process. The vision believes that the masses are capable of decision-making and define the government as a tool necessary for social control not engineering. The principle of limited government is fundamental because the Universal/Natural see government as a potentially evil institution. Separation of powers is thus used as a tool for counteracting tyranny and unchecked power. Federalism is paramount to balance out the scope, power and size of the national government. Civil rights and liberties are seen as something beyond the control and scope of the government, not as something the government gives to individuals through legislation and judicial activism. In fact the Universal/Natural believe judicial constraint is necessary to prevent judges from legislating from the bench and circumventing the checks and balances of our constitutional system.

This is not to say the governmental institution should not become involved in changing the social climate of the nation through adherence to constitutional law. During the difficult times of the civil rights movement, Martin Luther King Jr. offered a good example of how the government institution can be used to press society forward: "Morality cannot be legislated, but behavior can be regulated. Judicial decrees may not change the heart, but they can restrain the heartless."

Another way to look at the differences between the two views is to apply them once again to the concepts of "Can I" and "Should I". "Can I" means an individual is told specifically by government law what they are allowed to do or not do behaviorally. "Should I" means an individual must decide for themselves what behaviors they think are appropriate based on the incentives and costs placed on these behaviors from the institutions of economy, religion, family and education. The social control placed on individual behavior by the incentives created by the other four social institutions is vital to the Universal/ Natural worldview. These institutions offer in effect a balanced society that best advances the civilization in the mind of the Universal/Natural vision. In essence the Universal/Natural mind set perceives a healthy society as one that has a 50/50 balance between the "Can I" and the "Should I".

In contrast, the Humanistic/Synthetic worldview places the "Can I" as the fundamental tool in developing society by using the governmental institution to answer all behavioral questions for the individual. The question of "Should I" comes into play for the Humanistic/Synthetic but only if the "Can I" have not been determined by the government. In this case, the "Should I" are not affected by the incentives or costs provided by the other four social institutions but are decided by the individual in any way they deem appropriate. Of course, this is allowed only until the government steps in and creates new laws to address what previously was not under their control.

Caution should be applied to this argument however because the "Can I" of the Humanistic/Synthetic can be made to look like "Should I" in order to confuse and appear as having a balanced ideology. Thomas S. Szasz defined the Humanistic/Synthetic worldview as it applies to government control with a different adaptation of "Should I": "If it's bad for you, it should be prohibited; if it's good for you, it should be required."

Social engineering is thus a primary thrust for the Humanistic/Synthetic worldview using the government as the tool for the creation of a society they perceive as the most beneficial. For those with the Universal/Natural vision, social engineering has limited benefits based on the costs imposed and can in fact be dangerous. The Universal/Natural mind perceives social advancement as being a systemic process where change is based on the interplay of all five institutions upon the independent decision making by the masses.

Another way to look at government control from both sides is to understand that the Universal/Natural mind holds the principles of popular sovereignty, limited government, separation of powers, federalism, and civil rights/ liberties with the highest of value. Using a simple statement and filling in the blanks can highlight the determination of value for specific concepts. The Universal/Natural love _____more then they hate _____. For example, the Universal/Natural love federalism more than they hate guns. Or, they love limited government more than they hate smoking. Some would even say they love civil liberties or freedom more than they hate motorcycle helmet laws.

The Humanistic/Synthetic does not hold the principles of government to the same standard. Because of this another simple statement can be utilized to outline their beliefs. The Humanistic/Synthetic hate _____ more than they love _____. For example, the Humanistic/Synthetic hate guns more than they love federalism. Or, they hate smoking more than they love limited government. Some would even say they hate motorcycle accidents more than they love civil liberties or freedom. As a rule of thumb, the Humanistic/Synthetic focus is on individuals first, then the society. While the Universal/Natural have a focus is on society first, followed by individuals in dealing with social issues.

Because of this, the Humanistic/Synthetic vision does not feel it is detrimental to society to use the governmental institution to pass laws to create a society that is in alignment with their worldview. It is important to note that for every law passed, a little more freedom is taken away from the individual. The Universal/Natural is very wary of this while the Humanistic/Synthetic seems to ignore this fact. Ronald Reagan spoke of this concept concerning the erosion of liberty:

> I hope we have once again reminded people that man is not free unless government is limited. There's a clear cause and effect here that is as neat and predictable as a law of physics: as government expands, liberty contracts.

We could apply the love/hate analogy to a quote by Sidney Hook. "War is an evil…it is always an evil. What is wrong is believing war is the only evil, or that it is the worst." In other words the Humanistic/Synthetic would say they hate war more than they love stopping evil while the Universal/Natural would say they love the freedom war secures more than they hate war.

In closing, the fundamental concept that freedom allows for choice which has costs is respected and applied by the Universal/Natural and blindly perceived as non-existent by the Humanistic/Synthetic. For example, the freedom to not wear a motorcycle helmet is a choice for an individual. Once the choice has been made however there is a cost, that being the higher chance of sustaining a head injury in the event of a crash. Another example would be the freedom to choose to dress inappropriately (outside the norm of acceptable attire) for a job interview with the cost of lowering one's chance of getting the job. There are other differing perceptions between the two perceptual realities on topics such as equality of results versus equality of process, justice served versus justice of process and property redistribution versus property rights just to name a few. We could continue with these differences indefinitely but hopefully the point has been made as to how each worldview perceives the role of government and the ramifications that differing perceptions have on the maintenance of civilization.

Government

Humanistic/Synthetic	Universal/Natural
Government is pivotal institution	Government is a necessary evil
Unlimited government	Limited government/ federalism
Representatives: superior decision makers	Representatives represent people
Masses are not capable of decision making	Masses capable of decision making
Government—tool for social engineering	All institutions offer incentives
Omnipotent moral busybodies	50/50—"Can I" and "Should I"
Legislate morality	Can't legislate morality
Government gives civil rights/liberties	Regulate behavior
"Can I" answers all behavioral questions	Change is systemic
If bad—prohibit	Laws cost freedom
If good—require it	As gov't expands, liberty contracts
Social engineering	Freedom = choices = costs
As government expands, liberty expands	

13

ECONOMY

"If competition has evils, it prevents greater evils…It is the common error of Socialists to overlook the natural indolence of mankind; their tendency to be passive, to be slaves to habit, to persist indefinitely in a course once chosen. Let them once attain any state of existence which they consider tolerable, and the danger to be apprehended is that they will thenceforth stagnate…Competition may not be the best conceivable stimulus, but it is at present a necessary one, and no one can foresee the time when it will not be indispensable to progress."
—John Stuart Mill

The second social institution within civilized society that worldviews have an impact on is the economic system. By economic system we are referring to the production, distribution and consumption of wealth in the form of goods and services. This definition is tempered by the fact that man has unlimited wants yet limited resources to satisfy his needs. Thus the economic institution is a system for trying to answer the difficult questions of what shall we produce, how will we produce it and for whom will it be produced. In short, an economic system is a system of sharing and accepting unequal dissemination.

A properly functioning economic institution is vital to the health of the society because the most important role for an economic system is to economize. By doing so, a society will create the highest standard of living for the most people. If the institution is faulty, not only can people suffer needlessly but they can die. Each worldview offers opposing perceptions on how best to operate the economy in the most productive way.

There are seven economic goals and five components of capitalism that promote social prosperity. Free market capitalism provides the mechanism that allows for these goals to properly function. The seven economic goals are as follows:

1. Economic freedom: Personal choice in economic decision making without government interference.

2. Economic efficiency: The wise use of resources in order to economize based on the decisions of millions of participants.

3. Economic equity: Fairness in sharing limited resources based on applying the rules of the game equally to all participants.

4. Economic security: Lowering the fear of adverse economic events.

5. Full employment: Maximum employment opportunities.

6. Price stability: Balanced inflation and security in expansion of the money supply.

7. Economic growth: An expanding economy where the "pie" continues to grow thus providing all participants a larger slice.

Capitalism or free enterprise is an economic structure where citizens are free to pursue their economic goals. In order for capitalism to thrive five components must be embraced.

1. Competition: The struggle to attract consumers which in turn increases quality and decreases costs.

2. Economic freedom: The free choice in deciding economic questions such as job choice, product choice and product production.

3. Voluntary exchange: Free trade for goods and labor.

4. Profit motive: The incentive and cost of productivity and efficiency.

5. *Private property:* The right for individuals to control their possessions as they wish.

The Universal/Natural worldview answers the question of how to share by giving individuals the choice through a market economy that uses prices to answer the questions of what, how and for whom. Incentives are created to be productive by the role of competition and profit, which is the cost of a market economy. Economic health is created as millions of decisions are made by individuals based on supply and demand that move limited resources to fill the most desired needs. Adam Smith described this as the "Invisible hand" that guides decisions to the most productive ends. The role of government in the economy should be limited to enforcing the rules and then leaving the market economy to function on its own in what Smith called "Laissez faire".

The Humanistic/Synthetic will argue that monopolies counteract the freedom of a market economy but nothing could be further from the truth. Individual economic freedom provided in a market economy creates the inability for abusive corporate monopolies to be present. Although it may look to some that a monopoly is present, the freedom to compete or dissolve the monopoly through economic decisions of the masses keeps monopolies at bay. Some natural, technological and geographical monopolies do exist that are an efficient part of the economy however.

Abusive corporate monopolies can only be advanced when the government institution becomes involved in a market economy as a result of creating laws or protections that foster the rise of such monopolies. In fact, the largest "monopolies" in the United States today are found in civil service and public education, both of which are controlled by government. The belief that a company like Microsoft is a monopoly is absurd. Nothing in a free market economy is keeping any individual from creating an operating system that beats Windows. Just because a company is large or has a significant market share does not make it a monopoly. In fact, Microsoft must watch its back everyday from the likes of companies such as Apple. In addition, if large size constitutes a monopoly, which by definition is unstoppable, why then have so many companies gone out of business that at one time dominated the marketplace?

For the Universal/Natural the market system allows for individual freedom that creates winners and losers through competition. This in turn produces a situation where incentives motivate individuals to strive through an entrepreneurial spirit of inventiveness to become winners. The result of this process is the emergence of an economy that continually improves for all its members because the incentives create productivity that economizes limited resources to the benefit of everyone.

An example can be given by asking a few rhetorical questions. Has the development of the computer offered technology that has enriched the lives of millions of people? Is the world better off because Bill Gates became involved in developing software to operate the computer? Did Bill Gates develop the software to operate computers because he wanted to enrich lives or was it because he could envision the opportunity for economic benefits in the form of profit from his hard work and technological prowess? In short, positive social change comes from a market system that has far reaching benefits beyond what can be envisioned for all members in the society.

Counter to the market system is the vision of the Humanistic/Synthetic as it applies to the economic institution. This worldview answers the question of how to share by giving the power of choice to the government through a command economy that uses central decision making to answer the questions of what, how and for whom. Incentives to be productive and competitive in order to economize by the role of profit are ignored and abhorred. Inefficiency is the result, and as such is the cost of a command economy. Economic health is lost as millions of decisions that are incapable of being made by central planning move limited resources to varying degrees of success.

The example of the inefficient communist economic system found in the now defunct Soviet Union shows the ills a command economy has on a society. An engineered economy creates a lack of drive because there are no incentives to motivate individuals to be inventive, economize and raise the standard of living for all members in the society. As the economy worsens at a geometrically increasing pace, the government finds that it can no longer even feed its people. As a result the government must abuse its power to a greater extent until the people find the situation so unpalatable they remove power they have given to the government and rise up to overthrow the tyranny. To highlight these thoughts one must ponder the following fact. Under the last Russian Czar, the Russian economy was a net exporter of wheat, but during the Cold War of the 1980's, the communist government of the Soviet Union had to ask the United States to sell it wheat in order to feed its people.

To better understand the Humanistic/Synthetic worldview of economics some questions need to be asked. When would a command economy develop the computer that offered technology enriching the lives of millions of people? When would society be enriched as the result of computer technology; sooner, later or never as the result of a command economy? If the leaders of a command economy decided and in fact had the knowledge to create computer technology, would they use it to better the society for all its members or to maintain their power and control over its citizens? Would the answers to the last three questions create inefficiencies in the command economy beyond what can be envisioned that would lower the standard of living for all its citizens? A fundamental concept needs to be stressed in order to see the difference between a market and command economy. The profit found in a market economy is less costly than the inefficiencies of a command economy.

A cornerstone of the Humanistic/Synthetic worldview is the principle of income redistribution by the government. They believe it is vital to equalize the economy by taking from those that have and giving to those who do not. This is done by the creation of social programs paid for through taxation above and beyond the necessary functions of government spelled out in constitutional form. This is counter to what R.F. Harrod reminds us: "The most basic law of economics, namely that one cannot get something for nothing." Even Thomas Jefferson voiced an opinion on taxation in the economy. "A wise and frugal government, which shall restrain men from injuring one another, shall leave them otherwise free to regulate their own pursuits of industry and improvement, and shall not take from the mouths of labor the bread it has earned."

In the words of Walter Williams, unchecked taxation for the purposes of income redistribution amounts to little more than government sponsored theft. In fact, the definition of theft is the taking of property without consent or in secretive manner. Clearly many of the ways in which we are taxed are far from openly visible. The concept of income redistribution is compounded by a two-fold problem that is attached to our government structure. (1) Politicians understand that votes can be bought and power can be held if they give people something for free. (2) Citizens have learned that they can vote themselves money by the passing of laws. When these two factors filter into our system of governance, the root causes for the demise of our Republic have taken hold. One only has to look at the Social Security and Medicare problems, food stamp fraud or the thousands of pork barrel spending projects to highlight the abuse.

Alexander Tytler warned us of the outcome of income redistribution applied by the Humanistic/Synthetic worldview at the voting booth:

> A democracy cannot exist as a permanent form of government. It can only exist until the voters discover that they can vote themselves largess from the public treasury. From that moment on, the majority always votes for the candidate promising the most benefits from the treasury with the result that a democracy always collapses over loose fiscal policy.

Included in this discussion of the Humanistic/Synthetics view on the economy is the discussion of Anti-Americanism or as some would call it anti-capitalism. Victor Davis Hansen once again digs to the root of the issue by stating that:

> Anti-Americanism is as deeply psychological as it is politically motivated. Many observers of the phenomenon have commented that such hostility, especially in Europe, arises out of envy and jealousy. Of course it does, but the animus is still deeper and all the more virulent because it is a war of the heart versus the head…Professed hatred toward America for millions too often cloaks an inner desire for the very culture of freedom, material security, and comfort of the United States.

Hansen offers up a useful example of the hypocrisy evident in the Anti-American worldview held by some that hold a humanistic/Synthetic vision:

> Tenured academics who send their kids to private schools, vacation in Europe, and live in tasteful tree-lined suburbs…damn the very institutions that have provided their universities with such bountiful capital to make their lives so comfortable. They are perennially unhappy because what they castigate has given them everything they treasure, and they are either too weak—or too human—to confess it.

Hansen continues:

> It is not surprising that those most critical of America are not the purported victims of its supposedly rapacious capitalist system—farm workers, car mechanics, or welders—but more often those in the arts, universities, media and government, who have the time and leisure to contemplate utopian perfection without firsthand and daily exposure to backbreaking physical labor, relentless bullies, or unapologetically violent criminals. For such people, the new prosperity does not bring a greater

appreciation of the culture that has produced it but rather enables a fanciful shift from thinking in the immediate and concrete to idle musings of the distant and abstract.

The Universal/Natural worldview opposes the overzealous use of government taxation and income redistribution. They believe as Ralph Waldo Emerson did: "The basis of political economy is non interference. The only safe rule is found in the self adjusting meter of supply and demand." For the Universal/Natural, prices set by supply and demand for transactions in the form of purchases or the trade off in cash between worker and employer are free exchanges between individuals based on the decisions millions of other individuals have made. The Humanistic/Synthetic see this independent process as one that favors business without taking into account the role individual freedom plays in deciding what to buy, where to buy it, when to buy it or who to work for to build it. A simple question will exemplify the argument. When was the last time you heard of someone being forced at gunpoint to buy a loaf of bread or go to work at the local McDonalds?

Sure, capitalism has by its very process the inherent look on the surface of disproportionate wealth; but this in itself does not show what happens in reality. The general quality of life and prosperity for all has and continues to increase due to the forces at play in a market economy. Just ask any Cuban why they are willing to risk their life by floating on an inner tube across the dangerous Florida Straights to get to America in lieu of staying in communist Cuba. They will say it is because of economic opportunity and freedom. Winston Churchill clearly articulated the perceptual differences between a market economy and a command economy: "The inherent vice of capitalism is the unequal sharing of blessings. The inherent virtue of socialism is the equal sharing of miseries." Even Richard Nixon sounded off on this argument: "Capitalism works better than it sounds, while socialism sounds better than it works."

Fredrich Hayek summed up the institutional perception of the Humanistic/Synthetic as it applies to economics:

One argument frequently heard is that the complexity of modern civilization creates new problems with which we cannot hope to deal effectively except by central planning. This argument is based on a complete misapprehension of the working of competition. The very complexity of modern conditions makes competition the only method by which a coordination of affairs can be adequately achieved.

Hayek continued his analysis:

There would be no difficulty about efficient control or planning were conditions so simple that a single person or board could effectively survey all the facts. But as the factors which have to be taken into account become numerous and complex, no one center can keep track of them. The constantly changing conditions of demand and supply of different commodities can never be fully known, or quickly enough disseminated by any one center.

Hayek understood that the central need for an effective economy was knowledge. The Universal/Natural perception agrees that knowledge is best economized by the utilization of it at its source, that being the individual closest to the decision. The Humanistic/Synthetic believe that elite individuals have the knowledge to create a master plan for the economy.

Milton Friedman also discusses the role of government in the economy:

Fundamentally, there are only two ways of coordinating the economic activities of millions. One is central direction involving the use of coercion—the technique of the army and of the modern totalitarian state. The other is voluntary, cooperation of individuals—the technique of the marketplace.

Friedman is not saying the government plays no role in the economy only that: "The role of government (in a free society)...is to do something that the market cannot do for itself, namely, to determine the rules of the game."

Lastly, a fundamental difference can be outlined between the two perceptions of economic institutional functioning. The Humanistic/Synthetic believe the rules should be changed by surrogate decision makers before, during and after the economic game has begun in order to create the economic outcomes they feel are in the best interest of society. The Universal/Natural worldview accepts the rules of the game based on constitutionally sound principles and believe they should be applied equally to all individuals in the economy. These economic rules as well as the rule of law must be applied equally to all participants without modification after the economic game has commenced. To highlight this, ask yourself a question. What would happen if during the Superbowl the Commissioner of the NFL changed the rules at halftime to help one team that was being badly beaten in order to make the game seem "better" or "more fair"? You are correct if you said that there would be demonstrations in the streets, especially in the town of the team that was winning. The social ramifications of this example are frightening and yet the current governmental institution continually interferes with the economic "game" with blind impunity.

Economy

Humanistic/Synthetic	Universal/Natural
Central decision making	Individual choice
Gov't answers, what, how, for whom	Market economy
Command economy	Prices answer, what, how, for whom
Incentives, profit, competition abhorred	Incentives, competition, profit
Inefficiency is cost of socialism	Economize limited resources
Income redistribution	Invisible hand
Increased taxation	laissez faire
Do not trust supply and demand	Trust supply and demand
Equal sharing of miseries	Unequal sharing of blessings
Central planners have knowledge	Knowledge economized at its source
Central direction using coercion	Free exchange
Government can change rules of game	Voluntary cooperation
Create new rules to procure outcomes	Gov't enforces rules of the game
Socialism sounds better than it works	Apply rules evenly to all. Capitalism works better than it sounds.

14

EDUCATION

"Human history becomes more and more a race between education and catastrophe."—H.G. Wells

The education institution is a tricky structure to define. To some it means a formal school system while to others it encompasses an individual path to intellectual, emotional and personal growth. Whatever definition one places on education, everyone agrees it is a necessary component to the health and vitality of civilization. In order for civilization to be maintained, it is fundamental that children and adults are exposed to and acquire the tools needed to become productive members of society. Without education, a culture will lose its base of knowledge and digress as this loss cripples its institutions.

In a simpler sense, children must be taught so they can adjust to change and survive within an ever expanding and dynamic world. Education is the institution that allows for meaningful transfer of knowledge and assimilation of the vital social values and principles that act as the glue to prevent the breakup of historically civilizing processes. The problem we are faced with is the application of education from the standpoint of the two worldviews.

For the Humanistic/Synthetic worldview, education is applied through a governmental school system that controls and applies its perceptual ideology to the curriculum. This methodology is one that embraces every aspect of the Humanistic/Synthetic worldview that has been discussed at length in this text. As a result, children and adults are indoctrinated into a singular way of understanding how the world works. In short, the educational institution of the Humanistic/Synthetic is one in which individuals are told what to think.

Victor Davis Hanson exemplifies the current school climate in his book: *Between War and Peace.*

> We live in a society in which playground fights in our schools are now often adjudicated by concepts such as "zero tolerance" and "equal culpability." Rather than exercising moral judgment—and investing time and energy in such investigation our school principals simply expel any student caught fighting, as if the bully and his victim occupy the same moral ground.

Hanson continues by stating that:

> Our schoolbooks devote more space to Hiroshima than to the far greater casualties on Okanawa...Rather than do the hard work of learning about the historical relationships, conflicts, and similarities between Islamic culture and Christian culture, East and West, and Europe and Asia, our teachers simply avoid the trouble. They claim that all cultures are just "different", and thereby hope to avoid the hard and unpleasant questions that might prompt hurt feelings and eventual enlightenment, rather than jeopardize their own immediate raises and promotions...Teachers, professors, and reporters embrace such dubious notions because they bring either rewards or at least the satisfaction of being liked and in the majority...It is also less demanding to watch television than to read, safer to blame or praise both than investigate the culpability of one, neater to create rather than recall facts, and better to feel good about oneself by adopting platitudes of eternal peace and universal tolerance than to talk honestly of evil, war, and the tragic nature of man.

Hanson also discusses the Humanistic/Synthetic worldview as it applies to the curriculum with a keen observation as to the harm that is taking place within our public schools:

> Moral equivalence, conflict-resolution theory, utopian pacifism, and multiculturalism are, of course, antirational and often silly. But we should also have the courage to confess that they bring on, rather than avoid, conflict and killing, and breed rather than eradicate ignorance. In short, they are not ethical ideas at all but amoral in every sense of the word.

Government controlled schools have evolved into a bureaucratic monster that is only concerned with holding on to power and control over the billions

of dollars flowing into its coffers. As in all government run enterprises, inefficiency is the norm and thus the education of children becomes secondary to
job security and the maintenance of the status quo through "iron clad" tenure
and union domination. As a result, accountability and achievement becomes
something to avoid instead of something to strive for.

This methodology creates an education system that perpetuates cognitive
retardation. Individuals are not allowed to move through the developmental
process of acquiring an understanding of the two worldviews and independently deciding what they believe and how their beliefs should be applied to
the greater society. Over time this type of education institution feeds off its
own ignorance, slowly destroying itself and the society it is supposed to support from within.

Barbara W. Tuchman discussed the demise of society by the mindless
result of the Humanistic/Synthetic perception of education:

> Wooden-headedness consists of assessing a situation in terms of precon-
> ceived notions while ignoring or rejecting any contrary signs. It is acting
> according to wish while not allowing oneself to be confused by facts.

In the Universal/Natural worldview, education is applied through a part-
nership of governmental, private, parochial, and home school systems. These
are combined with the fundamental teachings of the institutions of government, economy, family, and religion to create a broad perceptual ideology to
the life curriculum. As a result, children and adults are not indoctrinated into a
singular way of understanding how the world works but are given the tools to
utilize their brains in diverse ways. In short, the educational institution of the
Universal/Natural is one in which individuals are taught how to think. The
Universal/Natural view accountability and achievement gains as a fundamental engine that drives decisions within the educational institution. Additionally, they believe the education institution must work closely with the family
institution at the local level to align curriculum with the needs of the community.

The end result is a system that perpetuates systematic cognitive growth.
This allows individuals to move through the developmental process of acquiring an understanding of worldviews to become individual citizens that respect
how their thoughts and actions fit into the context of the greater society. This
creates an education institution that supports growth not only in the individual but in the society as well, thus allowing for civilization to continue to sup-

port itself as well as advance. In short, ideals guide the Humanistic/Synthetic education system while truth directs the Universal/Natural.

Herbert Spencer voiced the Universal/Natural worldview in his analysis of education's role as an institution:

> Education…is closely associated with change, is its pioneer, is the never-sleeping agent of revolution, is always fitting men for higher things and unfitting them for things as they are. Therefore between institutions whose very existence depends upon man continuing what he is and true education, which is one of the instruments for making him something other than he is, there must always be enmity.

Spencer's words underscore the role of the education institution as the great moderator of the institutions of civilization. Its role is to allow for individuals to attain the analytical skills necessary to embrace institutions on the one hand while carefully watching them on the other; always mindful of their precarious role to act as pillars or cancers of civilization.

Alfred North Whitehead offered thoughts on the role education institutions play in maintaining society. "Education is the guidance of the individual towards a comprehension of the art of life; and by the art of life I mean the most complete achievement of varied activity expressing the potentialities of that living creature in the face of its actual environment." Whitehead's thoughts encompass the perceptual expression of the Universal/Natural worldview applied to education. He offers a model of education that embraces the broadest of intellectual pursuits that is constrained by the confines of man's limited potential working in an environment that is beyond his mastery.

It is clear that for the Humanistic/Synthetic vision education is a means to a utopian end. While the vision of the Universal/Natural sees education as a means to the best possible world based on a trade off created between reasoned men and a vast incomprehensible world of universal proportions. An anonymous quote sums up the divergent views on education in a profoundly philosophical way. "Liberals have more questions than answers; conservatives have more answers than questions."

Victor Davis Hansen offers a suggestion to help refocus our public education system towards a more productive and protective system for the maintenance of civilization:

> I would prefer that our government instruct Americans about the exceptional history of America, reinaugurate civic education in the schools,

explain that racism, sexism, and prejudice are endemic in the human species—but under the American system of government can be identified, discussed, and then ameliorated. If we could instill in our citizens a tragic rather than therapeutic sense of the world, they would understand that utopia is not possible on this earth but that the Constitution and institutions of the United States are mans best hope for eradicating the evil and ignorance that plague us all. If we could do all that, then Americans might project a sense of self confidence in their history and values that would admonish others that we are proud of, rather than ashamed of, being different—and that we care far more about the principles for which we fight than the applause of the day from the fickle, insecure, and mixed up.

The American system of government run schools is in a state of total collapse. The Humanistic/Synthetic vision has control over our schools and thus the blame must be placed squarely upon their watch. If the education institution is to survive, some fundamental changes must be made in order to realign education's purpose with its behavior in operating the public schools. The following is a partial list of reforms aligned with the principles of the Universal/Natural vision. These ideas run counter to the current methodology for public school operation held by the Humanistic/Synthetic.

* Increase expectations for students, teachers and school administrators.
* Provide a substantive liberal arts curriculum to all students. Stress reading, writing and arithmetic.
* Teach how to think, not what to think.
* Give parental freedom through school choice, vouchers, charter schools and local control.
* End the monopoly over our schools held by the teachers unions.
* Open up the teaching profession through alternative certification to those people who have expertise and a desire to teach.
* Remove political correctness and bias in textbooks.
* End the Goals 2000, School to Work and outcome based education curriculum.
* Increase standards, accountability and discipline for students, teachers and school administrators.
* Demand fiscal responsibility in spending and taxation.

* Work to end educational programs from special interest groups and legislative mandates that serve to set social values on children.

* Reform colleges of education to create teacher training programs that focus on content mastery not untested theoretical pedagogy.

* End the misuse of labels on children's abilities or inability's.

* Use standardized tests to determine if learning is taking place for all students.

* End the soft bigotry of low expectations for traditionally underachieving students.

* Install systematic phonics instruction in the early grades.

* Demand appropriate behavior and dress from students.

* Infuse the concepts of free enterprise into the public school institution.

* Use technology prudently as a tool for learning not an end-all solution.

* Look to compress the number of years of learning by teaching more in a shorter time focusing on mastery learning.

* End the practice of grade inflation.

* Stop social promotion.

* Turn back the polarizing movements of multiculturalism and diversity education.

* End the promotion of psychotropic drugs given to control children.

* Stop using schools as a social welfare agency, pharmacy and health care facility.

* Teach penmanship to our youngest learners.

* Look for alternative ways to enhance the monetary rewards of the teaching profession.

* End bilingual programs that do not have an accelerated exit methodology.

* Love children enough to do what is right, not what feels the best.

Education

Humanistic/Synthetic

Idealistic
Government controlled
Narrow perceptual ideology
Teach what to think
Cognitive retardation
Hardheaded
Preconceived notions
Means to utopian ends
More questions than answers
Act according to wish
Don't be confused with facts
Iron clad tenure
Union domination
Status quo

Universal/Natural

Truth/fact based
Educate from all institutions
Broad perceptual ideology
Teach how to think
Cognitive growth
Guards institutional corruption
The art of life
Learn potential within constraints
More answers than questions
Reform

15

FAMILY

"A home is not mere transient shelter: its essence lies in its permanence, in its capacity for accretion and solidification, in its quality of representing, in all its details, the personalities of the people who live in it."—H.L. Mencken

The institution of family as it applies to worldview understanding is a fairly straight proposition. Before we move to detail the differences between the two worldviews, let us first set some definitions of the family institution. The family institution is the method a civilized society uses to reproduce offspring that will be cared for and raised in an environment that is conducive to the developmental health of not only the child but to the society that the child must assimilate into. Clearly, raising children in the wild is far different from rearing them in a home. The defined structure of family is thus a necessity to the health and vitality of a society.

With that said, the two worldviews have different perceptions on how to apply their vision to the family institution. The Humanistic/Synthetic worldview perceives the family as any number of diverse relationships between pairs of humans or autonomous individuals. For them the family might be two women, two men, or one man or woman. These people may be single, married, life partners, divorced, aunts, uncles, grandparents or even children. In other words, parenting and family for the Humanistic/Synthetic can be anything an individual decides to define and create.

Even the methodology of reproduction is left up to the discretion of the individual. Surrogate mothers, adoption, in vitro fertilization and perhaps cloning are seen as tools to be used to create life. Even the decision to abort life is held as sacred ground by the Humanistic/Synthetic to be used based solely on individual choice. The Humanistic/Synthetic perceptual reality does not seem to realize that choices that are a part of individual freedom have costs. The free choice to engage in reproductive behavior is not the problem. The problem is a worldview that believes the cost of their actions, notably becoming pregnant, can be ignored after the fact. This is no different than stabbing someone with a knife and then going to court and telling the judge "You can't put me in jail because I was just expressing my individual freedom of choice." My guess is that the judge would not see it that way because freedom comes with a cost.

In the home of the Humanistic/Synthetic, parenting styles tend to be permissive in accordance with the worldview of the parental unit in charge of raising the child. In his book "The Moral Sense", James Q. Wilson quotes a study of student activists done by Stanley Rothman and S. Robert Lichter that helps to explain how differing family structures can lead to social activism and a Humanistic/Synthetic world view. Wilson reports:

> Young people who had the most extreme views during the 60's scored at least one standard deviation above the mean on a "New Left Ideology" test. Not surprisingly, the need for power among this group was high. The radical activists described their parents as being emotionally distant and their upbringing as being coldly permissive. There is not much evidence here of students suffering from an excessively cruel conscience instilled by an overly authoritarian father; on the contrary, political extremism in this group was associated with uncaring parents who were permissive, not out of fondness, but out of indifference.

Russel Kirk adds to this discussion in describing the Humanistic/Synthetic vision of family:

> The alternative to the vigorous family is universal orphanage. If the family disintegrates, there remain only two modes of human existence. The first of these is an atomic individualism, every man and woman isolated and self-seeking. The result is adventitious and yet transitory. The second is that of total individualism, which is the negation of society that brings about compulsory collectivism. In the second there exists freedom of a sorts, but it is what John Adams called the freedom of the wolf, as distinguished from the moral freedom of the truly human person.

Wilson and Kirk's analysis shows the ramifications for civilized existence by the erosion of fundamental family elements that comes from a Humanistic/Synthetic worldview. What all of this adds up to is a family institution that is truly synthetic and counter to the natural order of reproduction and child rearing that is essential to the maintenance of civilization. The intentions are noble under the Humanistic/Synthetic perception of family, but the ability to raise a child outside of the laws of nature which prescribe the necessary elements to incorporate what is best for the child is lost.

So how does the Universal/Natural perceive the family institution? They see the family as a unit consisting of a mother and father, bound by a symbolic social contract to reproduce and raise children together. This union is in charge of administering the lessons and social constructs necessary to create productive and civil members of society in accordance with civil and natural law.

John Locke detailed the importance of the family institution and its vital role to the maintenance of civilization:

> The power, then, that parents have on children, arises from that duty which is incumbent on them, to take care of their offspring, during the imperfect state of childhood. To inform the mind, and govern the actions of their yet ignorant nonage, till reason shall take its place, and ease them of that trouble, is what the children want, and parents are bound to: for God having given man an understanding to direct his actions, has allowed him a freedom of will, and liberty of acting, as properly belonging thereunto, within the bounds of that law he is under...the nourishment and education of their children is a charge so incumbent on parents for their children's good, that nothing can absolve them from taking care of it.

There will be situations, of course, that will create family structures that are at odds with the aforementioned ideal situation. Obviously, there will be cases where there is the death of a spouse or the necessity of divorce as a result of abuse or danger to the children. In these situations, the raising of a child is not within the ideal range and a best case scenario can only be hoped for as a result. These realities however should not open up the door of legitimacy for any and all family structures defined by the Humanistic/Synthetic worldview. In fact, the lackadaisical attitude towards divorce currently underway in society and promoted by the doctrine of the Humanistic/Synthetic is impacting children in a profound way.

The reason for the high divorce rate and apathy towards the family institution is the result of a Humanistic/Synthetic worldview that embraces individual autonomy first. Parents view their personal happiness over the needs of their children and feel entitled to leave a marriage if and when they feel it does not suit their needs. Children are seen as trophies for the Humanistic/Synthetic worldview where personal responsibility is trumped by individual feelings. Contrary to this view, the Universal/Natural vision embraces children first and places their personal happiness in a secondary role to the magnificent responsibility they have been blessed with.

It is clear that a child raised as the result divorce is effected by the environmental changes that take place. In fact, the death of a parent is less damaging to a child than divorce, as the death can be far more easily reconciled as opposed to the abandonment issues felt as the result of divorce. Striving for the Universal/Natural worldview as it applies to the family institution offers the greatest opportunity for maximizing the chance that children will be raised with their biological mother and father.

The Universal/Natural perception views reproduction with the highest of respect. Procreation is seen as a behavior that is accountable and thus comes with responsibility. Even the decision to abort life is understood to be counter to the moral truths held dearly by the Universal/Natural vision. In the home of the Universal/Natural couple, parenting styles tend to be authoritative and cooperative in accordance with the perceptions of their worldview.

Because of these factors, the child raised under the Universal/Natural worldview has the best chance of developing in harmony with the natural order of reproduction and child rearing that is essential to the maintenance of the civilization. The end result is a family institution that understands and works in accordance with the laws of nature by proscribing the values and social lessons necessary to uphold and advance civilization. Situations are never perfect, but ignoring the family institution because it must work within the laws of a fallible human nature harms children. For that reason only, the nuclear family must be maintained.

Allan Bloom defines the Universal/Natural family:

> The family requires the most delicate mixture of nature and convention, of human and divine, to subsist and perform its function. Its base is merely bodily reproduction, but its purpose is the formation of civilized human beings.

Kate Millet has also chimed into the family institution argument. Her analysis may be confused by her attack on men that may be a vestige of her worldview development, but she rightly outlines the important role of the family institution:

> Patriarchy's chief institution is the family. It is both a mirror of and a connection with the larger society; a patriarchal unit within a patriarchal whole. Mediating between the individual and the social structure, the family affects control and conformity where political and other authorities are insufficient…serving as an agent of the larger society, the family not only encourages its own members to adjust and conform, but acts as a unit in the government of the patriarchal state which rules its citizens through its family heads.

To summarize; family is an open ended game for the Humanistic/Synthetic worldview, while it is seen as a humbling responsibility for those with a Universal/Natural worldview. When it is easier to renounce a marriage than a mortgage and when parental notification is needed in order for a child to pierce their bodies but is not necessary to have an abortion; the family institution is clearly on shaky ground.

Family

Humanistic/Synthetic	Universal/Natural
Any diverse relationship	Nuclear family = man and woman
Reproductive freedom	Symbolic social contract
Permissive parenting style	Authoritative parenting style
Synthetic family institution	Administer lessons, social constructs
Raise child outside laws of nature	Respect for procreation
Universal orphanage	Abortion versus natural laws
Atomistic individualism	Formation of civilized humans
Compulsory collectivism	Mediates individual/social structure
Open ended game	Affects control and conformity
	Agent of larger society
	Humbling responsibility

16

RELIGION

"Religion is not a hobby or passing fancy, it is an instrumental part of what the founders saw as a necessary part to a civilization that would flourish." To ignore this is to say you don't believe in a civilization."—Stephen Carter

The last institution we need to connect to the binary worldviews is that of religion. The nature of any discussion on religion brings with it an uncomfortable aura to many. However, if we are to be complete in applying the worldviews to better understand how our perceptions influence our civilization, we must proceed with an open mind.

With that said, what defines the institution of religion in society? Webster's dictionary defines religion as "a specific system of belief or worship of God or gods often involving a code of ethics." In America, we have a predominantly Judeo-Christian faith system but the entire range of accepted world religions are represented within this discussion. What's important is not the specific religion practiced, but the practice of a system of beliefs that carry with them a moral code of conduct. This code is not based on individually defined morality, but a morality based on universally agreed upon moral absolutes common to all world religions. In fact, James Q. Wilson has pointed out universal rules of moral behavior that have been found across all cultures including those against incest and against homicide in the absence of defined excusing conditions.

One of the problems many run into in regard to accepting religion is connecting religion with a specific church or religious order. Organized religion does play the pivotal role in providing the methodology from which one can

135

gain an understanding of the teaching and practices that brings one to live under a moral code. But it is not a necessity to go to church to understand the teaching and practices and then live according to their precepts. Fellowship may be beneficial and preferable to help some grow mentally in a theological sense and there is no problem in doing so. But it is also just as important to point out that just because someone attends a place of worship does not automatically make them fully aware of the worldview of the Universal/Natural perception. In the final analysis, living in accord with God's teachings is a personal relationship between an individual and God based on faith, trust, hope acceptance and love.

Within the context of civilization, the religious institution functions as a mechanism to answer the unanswerable questions of the universe to a curious and reasoning man in search for deeper meaning of life and beyond. In addition, the religious institution provides a template for moral behavior in order for humans to live together and flourish. The role of the institution is to stand alone in a philosophical realm that the other institutions of civilized society do not emphasize. The unique difference of the religious institution is that costs associated with making poor decisions come after one is no longer living. Because the incentives offered by the religious institution in guiding the "Should I's" do not have consequences in the here and now; the Humanistic/Synthetic ignore the ramifications inherent in being guided by such an institution.

In simpler terms, religion answers the question of "Should I" or "May I" in a moral sense. The religious institution does this because the other institutions may offer incentives based on "Can I" or through costs associated with poor decisions relating to the "Should I" incentives the institutions provide in the here and now. The fundamental question in guiding man's behavior from the religious standpoint is based on asking oneself, what would God want us to do? The answers to the wide range of questions queried to God are intangible and based purely on faith alone. This is what separates religion from the other institutions and why its role is so important.

The problem lies when one looks to comprehend religion from the Humanistic/Synthetic worldview. The reason for this is because the Humanistic/Synthetic worldview is secular (non-religious) in nature. The vision regards religion as outside the box of reasoned thought and thus is an antiquated notion. In this regard, Edmond Burke countered the Humanistic/Synthetic mind set: "Show me an absurdity in religion, and I will undertake to show you a hundred in political laws and institutions."

In effect then, the Humanistic/Synthetic mind lives in a world of moral relativity and secular humanism where individual behavior is anything they deem acceptable. Behavioral decisions are based in terms of "Can I" only, while the "Should I" component of individual control is ignored.

The bottom line in understanding the problem between the secular society of the Humanistic/Synthetic and the religious one of the Universal/Natural is really is a simple and fundamental question of perspective and vision as to how the world works. Do you believe in a power greater than self or not? If the answer is yes, you have the foundation of faith that allows one to begin the process of spiritual guidance that accepts the religious institution as legitimate. The Universal/Natural believes in a power greater than self while the Humanistic/Synthetic struggle with having a complete acceptance to this question.

James Madison spoke of the role of religion on civilization:

> It is the duty of every man to render to the Creator such homage, and such only, as he believes to be acceptable to him. This duty is precedent both in order of time and degree of obligation, to the claims of Civil Society. Before any man can be considered as a member of Civil Society, he must be considered as a subject of the Governor of the Universe.

Stephen Carter's: *The Culture of Disbelief has* analyzed the most profound questions as they apply to the religious institution in society. He discusses the Humanistic/Synthetic as well as the Universal/Natural perceptions of religion in a wide range of topics. Carter exposes the secular nature of the Humanistic/Synthetic worldview:

> More and more our culture seems to take the position that believing deeply in the tenets of one's faith represents a kind of mystical irrationality, something that thoughtful, public spirited American citizens would do better to avoid...Religion is more and more treated as passing beliefs, almost fads, rather than the fundamentals upon which people build their lives. If your beliefs are inconvenient then give them up or alter them...Culture in effect says pray and worship if you must but do not on any account take your religion seriously...Moral truths when justified by religious doctrine are treated as hack intellectualism in today's public debate. All "proper" views must be made based on secular terms or they are attacked.

Carter also describes the perceptions of the Universal/Natural worldview towards religion:

> Society in general does not understand that people have the need to have their lives make sense and to transcend the dynamics of individualism and selfishness that predominate our social fabric…Maybe the popular culture does not want to feel uncomfortable when faced with thinking about the ultimate questions of the universe and thus it is easy to just censor any talk about God so they can get on with their lives.

> Science can't be used as a superior tool to understand the truths of the universe for it is a tool to understand the natural world whereas religion is a system based on faith about truths beyond the natural world. Moral claims unlike factual claims do not rely for their validity on the generation of testable hypotheses.

The importance of the religious institution within a framework of all of the institutions working together in a productive way is also examined. Steven Carter exemplifies the caution found in the Universal/Natural mind as it applies to institutional power and balance:

> The religious institution provides the moral framework and the mitigating necessity in which democracy needs to function under. Without it the government will fill the void with its view of ultimate truths…Respect for religious autonomy demands a respect for that group activity of searching. The fear in popular culture is that the group searching for ultimate meaning might find it and having found it the group might place it at the center of their conceptual universe where it will displace the competing claims for ultimate meaning that are made by that powerful agglomeration of individuals known as the state.

Carter continues:

> The religious institution says that man will not "accede to your will" for god is above you and that power you may try to hold over me is trumped by a higher authority. God is superior to the state (Government) and if we lose, that the state could and many times has fallen into tyranny. The state should not control religion and religion should not control the state.

Thus, the group who searches for meaning becomes for its members the source of sense and value and authority that will supersede the state. This tension creates the need for the state or popular culture to impose a set of meanings or truths on the world that supersedes individual consciousness.

Allowing the courts to decide all the tough questions treats religion with disdain and as an institution of lesser importance, a dangerous road if our civilization is to survive.

Carter's analysis stands on its own clarity and reason. The Humanistic/ Synthetic worldview dismisses the religious institution because they do not have the cognitive capacity to process and articulate a set of principles they can't see, are intangible and are blind to because they are highly difficult to ascertain.

On a more positive note, many Humanistic/Synthetic minds are forced to begin the transformation into the Universal/Natural frame of mind as they are confronted with a great loss in their life. The grieving process that emerges as a result of loss has 5 stages: denial, anger, bargaining, depression and acceptance of the loss. In order to move past stage three, one will have to bargain with a higher power. Thus, in order to move through the grieving process and accept a loss, individuals must undertake a cognitive exercise through the religious institution. Looking at the difficulty the Humanistic/Synthetic have in coming to terms with religion may explain why they are often in denial or angry?

There are four tenets of the religious institution that are used by each worldview in different ways. They are individual consciousness, tolerance, religious diversity and religious passion. Lets examine each of them within their respective worldview to gain a better understanding of the social schism that religion creates.

1. Individual consciousness. The Universal/Natural define this to mean ones religiously spiritual thought must be respected and allowed to operate in freedom so as to function in word and deed openly. The Humanistic/Synthetic apply this to mean that whatever an individual believes is justifiable and off limits to debate and judgment. Religious freedom can be taken away if and when they deem it appropriate.

2. Tolerance. The Universal/Natural define this to mean that respect for religious practices as well as secular pursuits must be given. For the Humanistic/ Synthetic tolerance means being tolerant only as long as one wishes to show tolerance. Tolerance must be shown only to the ideals they view as acceptable. This is the type of tolerance the secular humanists use to muffle religious and spiritual thought within the social framework.

3. *Religious diversity.* The Universal/Natural define this as a respect for the many roads to God and a higher understanding of moral truths that are applied to behavior. The Humanistic/Synthetic define diversity as a notion that is used to protect the secular society from the religious one. They use the cry for diversity as a reason to legitimize any and all secular lifestyles. Diversity is a defense used to keep religion away from the social framework the Humanistic/Synthetic has defined as a "religious free zone".

4. *Religious passion.* The Universal/Natural define this to mean one's outward expressions of a spiritual nature should be respected. Additionally, they believe that one does not have the right to kill for ones beliefs only the right to die for them. For the Humanistic/Synthetic, passion is seen as an infraction on one's rights not to be bothered by religious expressions in words or deeds.

In closing, two quotes convey the majesty the religious institution plays in man's existence and the moral indignation of following blind perceptions. George Washington gave his thoughts concerning religion's necessity:

> Let us with caution indulge the supposition that morality can be maintained without religion. Reason and experience both forbid us to expect that national morality can prevail in exclusion of religious principle. Religion is as necessary to reason as reason is to religion. The one cannot exist without the other.

Eric Fromm highlighted the Humanistic/Synthetic vision concerning morality without a religious base:

> There is perhaps no phenomenon that which contains so much destructive feeling as "moral indignation," which permits envy or hate to be acted out under the guise of virtue. The "indignant" person has for once the satisfaction of despising and treating a creature as "inferior," coupled with the feeling of his own superiority and rightness.

Religion

Humanistic/Synthetic	Universal/Natural
Secular humanism	Religious institution paramount
Antiquated notion	Code of ethics/moral conduct
Moral relativity	Organized religion = methodology
Behavior is up to the individual	Relationship—individual and God
Behavior based on "Can I"	Answers unanswerable questions
No power greater than self	Belief in power greater than self
Institution is not legitimate	Answers "Should I's"
Mystical irrationality	What would God want us to do
Don't take your religion seriously	Accepts spiritual guidance
Hack intellectualism	Institution is legitimate
Attack all non secular views	Transcends individualism
Uncomfortable with ultimate questions	Cant test morals through science
Science is superior tool	Respects religious autonomy
Fear religion will define truth	God is above the state
Judgments not allowed	Source of sense and values
Tolerance only to ideals they accept	Respect individual consciousness
Muffle religious thoughts in society	Respect religious tolerance
Diversity of secular lifestyles	Respect religious diversity
Passion is infraction to one's rights	Respect religious passion
Kill for secular beliefs	Die for ones beliefs/principles
No responsibility to die for principles	Religion maintains morality
Religion is not necessary for reason	Religion is necessary to reason
Moral indignation	

IV
DECISIONS

17

SUMMARY AND
CONCLUSIONS

"The final decision as to the future of a society depends not on how near its organization is to perfection, but on the degrees of worthiness in its individual members."—Albert Schweitzer

As you begin reading the final chapter of this journey into worldview development, some perceptual decisions need to be made. Hopefully the analysis and theory that has been presented will be cause for some personal reflection and possibly a reordering of perceptions of how you view the world. The realization of your worldview, be it Universal/Natural, Humanistic/Synthetic or a transitional combination of the two should give rise to at least a higher level of cognitive understanding. Additionally, gaining a more advanced understanding of the two worldviews will allow for empathetic and intuitive debate. If this has been accomplished then the effort has been a success.

So where do you go from here? For some, this is just another of a long list of readings you have undertaken to better understand the world of the social sciences. For others, this may have been your first journey into the workings of man and society. The most important thing however is that the intellectual pursuit must continue. One must think and express their views through an intellectual prism that is based on a true understanding of how and why they think as they do. Blind perceptions and the associated misdirection of knowledge has no place in critical thought. Knowledge is power and opening one's eyes to the realities of the human dynamic will allow for individuals to join in the debate with a clear perspective. Hopefully the information provided will add to the discussion in order to move social rhetoric forward in a productive way.

The lack of intellectual consistency that dominates the public argument must be replaced with sound reasoning and an understanding of the workings of civilization as well as the visions man has towards society. Blind perceptions of one's worldview are dangerous and quite possibly fatal to the social fabric we are entrusted to maintain. Apathy and indifference to what people are thinking and acting upon will not advance civilization. Stephen Covey articulated what must take place if America is to retain its glory and survive as a society that would make the founders proud. "If we want to change a situation, we first have to change ourselves. And to change ourselves effectively, we first have to change our perceptions."

On the surface, or in theory, the Humanistic/Synthetic worldview looks to be an accurate and appropriate mechanism for social advancement while the Universal/Natural seems to be out of step. In practice however, the Humanistic/Synthetic worldview is inefficient and dangerous while the Universal/Natural worldview is the most efficient and beneficial mechanism for social advancement for all members off society.

With that said, an attack on the doctrine of the Humanistic/Synthetic is not what is needed even though the vision should cause alarm to those who care about the maintenance of civilization. The worldview of the Humanistic/Synthetic is not going to suddenly end as it is a part of the developmental process in humans. What needs to be realized however is that the Humanistic/Synthetic vision is at an early stage of perceptual reality. Those at this stage must continue their advancement because they just don't fully understand the dynamics of humanity. Dr. Phillip McGraw often tells his guests on television: "You just don't seem to understand, that is not how the world works." In essence he is saying that the psyche of some individuals has not yet come to accept the reality of life on a sphere called Earth floating in a vast universe. The most important question that needs to be asked as we contemplate the maintenance of civilization is, are you part of the problem or a part of the solution?

Incivility is permeating our society. The cause of which can be traced to the breakdown of the institutions that maintain civility. The current issue that is causing the decline of our civilization can be traced to a Humanistic/Synthetic vision that is beginning to dominate our society. This is a problem because the vision has less validity in action than the Universal/Natural worldview but acts as if it has all the answers. We must recognize this situation as a course that our civilization must not take. The balance that arises between the two world-views is a healthy one as long as we realize the stages of worldview development incorporate vastly differing perceptions that can lead to social destruction. Therefore, we must ascribe differing amounts of legitimacy to each worldview's ability to maintain civilization. This is not to say the Universal/Natural worldview should prevail without constraints because if we have learned one thing it is that linear visions can be dangerous. It must however take a dominant role in guiding social change.

Unfortunately, institutional decline may be in fact something that man cannot overcome. The reason for this may be the result of the lethal combination of human nature and the bureaucratic inefficiencies inherent in institutions. As vital institutions are built they have a tendency to grow beyond their original scope and power. As an outcome of this growth the original intent institutions were founded upon is lost as their basic principles and organizational structure slowly turn 180 degrees. There are far too many historic examples of institutions that evolved into powerful forces that undermined the very civilization they were built to sustain. A close look at the governmental, religious, family, education and economic institutions in the United States reveals a system that in many respects is the antithesis of that which the founders created and envisioned.

The United Nations is a good example of an institution growing past its usefulness and shifting in focus away from the very principles upon which it was founded. When Libya, a country that is known for its human rights violations and state sponsored terrorism under leaders like Kadaffi is in charge of the United Nations Human Rights Commission, we all must give pause to the inability of institutions to maintain their original purpose. What was once an organization founded to secure freedom and fundamental universal values has turned into what many have called a "debating society" that is incapable of securing and promoting even the most basic principles of civilized existence.

Today in America the governmental institution has evolved into an entity that controls freedom instead of protecting it. The economic institution is evolving into an entity that controls the market instead of allowing it to operate in freedom. The religious institution is evolving into an entity that seeks to control ones relationship with God instead of allowing the freedom of faith. The education institution has evolved into an entity that controls thought instead of allowing freedom of thought. Lastly, the family institution has evolved into an entity that has lost control and replaced it with the freedom of moral equivalency in personal choice.

It is quite possible that institutional collapse is inherent in mans limited capacity to control his very nature. The best rule of thumb applied to institutions to stem the tide of bureaucratic collapse would be to control their growth. Clearly, when it comes to man building institutions and organizations, smaller is better. Hopefully the underlying purpose of this book will offer some insights into counteracting and slowing what may be an unstoppable process of the human condition.

The necessary balance between the two worldviews is being lost as the Humanistic/Synthetic worldview of secular humanism and government control becomes more commonplace. This is being accomplished slowly and quietly by geometrically increasing ignorance due to the fact that each successive generation is less able to clearly perceive the vital principles necessary for civil society. James Madison warned of this eventuality: "There are instances of the abridgement of the freedom of the people by gradual and silent encroachments of those in power than by violent and sudden usurpations." It could be suggested that at the time of our nation's founding, most of the leadership were aligned with a Universal/Natural worldview that arose out of the classical liberalism of the enlightenment. Over time our nation achieved more of a balance between the two worldviews. Today that balance has been lost to Madison's gradual and silent encroachments.

When looking at the political arena, it may seem as if there is still a balance between the two worldviews. One look at the 2000 presidential election results would seem to suggest that the country is divided evenly among opposing views. But statistically speaking, only 66% of those able to vote register, and of the registered voters only about half or 33% of the eligible population actually vote. This would mean that in the 2000 election only 16.5% of eligible voters voted Republican while the other 16.5% voted Democrat. The key question we are faced with deals with the 66% of voting age Americans that go unaccounted for. Some would argue they are split evenly in their worldviews. Others would be more pessimistic and say a majority have been indoctrinated into a Humanistic/Synthetic worldview and are unable to grow beyond its precepts. Lastly, optimists would argue that a silent majority is firmly aligned with a Universal/Natural worldview but has been silenced by the encroachments of those in power that hold a Humanistic/Synthetic vision.

Another cause of imbalance stems from the fact that the Universal/Natural worldview by its very nature is passive and non-confrontational. Oppose this to the Humanistic/Synthetic worldview that uses emotional idealism that legitimizes the ends justifying the means and there is little wonder individuals are easily indoctrinated or misled into accepting the Humanistic/Synthetic worldview as accurate and beyond judgment. The mainstream media and the public schools are also to blame for the shift in balance between the world-views as they report and teach in unison from the perceptions of the Humanistic/Synthetic. Although a silent majority may in fact stand firmly with a Universal/Natural vision, if indeed everyone actually could articulate their beliefs, their lack of noise perpetuates the rise and control of the Humanistic/Synthetic.

Thomas Jefferson reminds us that there is a time when the people need to wake up and go into action:

> The people cannot be all, and always, well informed. The part which is wrong will be discontented in proportion to the importance of the facts they misconceive. If they remain quiet under such misconceptions, it is a lethargy, the forerunner of death to the public liberty.

Blind perceptions are creating a situation that is making institutions impotent. The continuation of this social methodology will in due time crush the independent nature in productive institutions until when civilization as we know it no longer exists.

So what can we do? Maybe a good place to start would be for those with the Humanistic/Synthetic worldview to stop their idealistic love affair with the governmental institution as a utopian end all and respect the role and importance the other institutions of civilized society play in moving our society forward. In doing so, common ground could be found to allow for the beginning of meaningful dialogue in order to save civilization from our self inflicted ignorance. In addition, it is imperative for those with the Universal/Natural worldview to stop sitting on the sidelines and begin to fight for their perceptions and principles. This may be uncomfortable at first but to remain silent is just not an option at this point. Thomas Jefferson was prophetic in his words discussing the maintenance of civilization in America and it under-scores the current crisis America faces:

> The spirit of the times may alter, will alter. Our rulers will become corrupt, our people careless. A single zealot may commence (as) persecutor, and better men be his victims. It can never be too often repeated that the time for fixing every essential right on a legal basis is while our rulers are

honest and ourselves united. From the conclusion of (their) war (for independence, a nation begins) going down hill. It will not then be necessary
to resort every moment to the people for support. They will be forgotten,
therefore, and their rights disregarded. They will forget themselves but in
the sole faculty of making money, and will never think of uniting to effect
a due respect for their rights. The shackles, therefore, which shall not be
knocked off at the conclusion of (that) war will remain on (them) long,
will be made heavier and heavier, till (their) rights shall revive or expire in
a convulsion.

Look around you, what do you see? What you see is a society that is out of
order and out of control. Our cultural fabric has become amoral, self-serving,
ignorant, abusive of power, void of leadership, secular, utopian, and discon-
nected from reasoned reality. When this is coupled with the deterioration of
the governmental, economic, religious, family and education institutions one
has plenty of reason for alarm. The cultural pot is quickly coming to a boil;
let's hope, like the proverbial frog, we realize it and feel the heat before it's too
late.

978-0-595-35992-9
0-595-35992-2

www.ingramcontent.com/pod-product-compliance
Lightning Source LLC
Chambersburg PA
CBHW022254290526
45785CB00015B/775